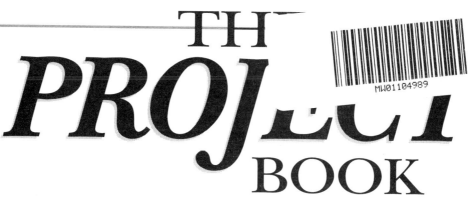

THE PROJECT BOOK

An Introduction to Research and Writing

Hugh Robertson

Cartoons by Cuyler Black

McGraw-Hill Ryerson Limited

Toronto   Montreal   New York   Auckland   Bogotá   Caracas   Lisbon   London   Madrid   Mexico
Milan   New Delhi   Paris   San Juan   Singapore   Sydney   Tokyo

The Project Book
An Introduction to Research and Writing

ISBN 0-07-551418-4

234567890 W 32109876

Printed and bound in Canada

Care has been taken to trace ownership of copyright material contained in this text. The publishers will gladly accept any information that will enable them to rectify any reference or credit in subsequent editions.

Canadian Cataloguing in Publication Data
Robertson, Hugh, date—
The project book: an introduction to research and writing

Includes bibliographical references.
ISBN 0-07-551418-4

1. Report writing — Juvenile literature
I. Black, Cuyler. II. Title.

LB1047.3.R63 1993 808'.02 C93-094459-3

Publisher: Janice Matthews
Associate Editor: Nancy Christoffer
Senior Supervising Editor: Carol Altilia
Permissions Editor: Crystal Shortt
Copy Editor: Geraldine Kikuta
Cover and Interior Design: Dave Hader/Studio Conceptions
Cover Illustration: Cuyler Black

This book was manufactured in Canada using acid-free and recycled paper.

Readers wishing further information on data provided through the cooperation of Statistics Canada may obtain copies of related publications by mail from: Publications Sales, Statistics Canada, Ottawa, Ontario, Canada K1A 0T6, by calling 1-613-951-7277 or toll-free 1-800-267-6677. Readers may also facsimile their order by dialing 1-613-951-1584.

CONTENTS

ACKNOWLEDGEMENTS v

1 INTRODUCTION 1

2 REPORTS 3

Research 4
   Selecting the Topic 4
   Narrowing the Focus 6
   Locating Sources 8
   Defining the Purpose 11
   Developing the Working Outline 12
   Recording Information 14

Presentation 17
   Shaping the Outlines 18
      Basic Outline 18
      Skeleton Outline 19
      Point-form Outline 20
   Rough Draft 22
      Paragraphing 22
      Drafting the Introduction 24
      Drafting the Body 25
      Drafting the Concluding Summary 26
   Final Copy 27
      Title Page 27
      Table of Contents 27
      Illustrations 28
      Appendix 28
      Documenting Sources 29
      Listing Sources 29

3 ESSAYS 31

Research 32
   Selecting the Topic 32
   Narrowing the Focus 33
   Locating Sources 34
   Defining the Purpose 37
   Recording Information 38
      Index Card Method 38
      Notepaper Method 41

Presentation 44
   Shaping the Outlines 45

Basic Outline 45
Skeleton Outline. 46
Point-form Outline 47
The Rough Draft 48
Drafting the Introduction 49
Drafting the Body 50
Drafting the Concluding Summary 51
Revising and Editing. 53
The Final Copy. 55
Quotations. 56
Documenting Sources. 57
Listing Sources. 59

4 COMPARATIVE ESSAYS **61**
Preparation. 63
Notepaper Method. 64
Index Card Method 66
Presentation. 67
Sample Essay 70

5 TIPS ON STYLE **73**

6 CONCLUDING SUMMARY. **75**

APPENDIX **77**
1. Oral Presentations 77
2. Multimedia Presentations. 79
3. Illustrations 80
Tables. 80
Figures 81
Maps. 81
Organizational Charts. 82
Line Graphs. 82
Bar/Column Charts 84
Circle Charts. 85
Climate Graphs. 86

GLOSSARY. **87**

ENDNOTES. **89**

BIBLIOGRAPHY. **90**

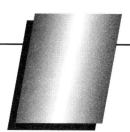

ACKNOWLEDGEMENTS

Many people have shared in developing *The Project Book*. I am indebted to the following for their comments and advice: Richard Baine, Tara Boyd, John Einarson, Christine Hammond, Mivi and Michael Jansen, Glen Kirkland, Mary McGuinness, and Mary Jane Pickup.

I am especially grateful to Stuart Grainger for his perceptive comments and practical suggestions. A special thank you to Matthew Labarge for his computer expertise and his endless reserves of good humour. I would also like to express my sincere thanks to Nancy Christoffer, whose editorial skills and wise counsel have helped shape *The Project Book.*

The process described in this guide has been developed and refined over many years of teaching at Ashbury College. To the students, staff, and administration, my grateful thanks for their support over the years. I would also like to acknowledge the efforts of four students who have assisted in preparing the sample assignments in the guide: Seth Glynn, Jonathan Lee, Darren Prevost, and Ian Quan.

INTRODUCTION

An explorer setting off on an expedition needs to pack provisions, a route map, and equipment such as a compass. When you start a research project, you also need to be prepared. This guide will provide you with the essentials for your backpack as well as a sense of direction.

The guide will take you step by step through a process for preparing and presenting reports and essays in both oral and written form. Although a report and an essay are different, the way you prepare and present them is similar. It is important that you work your way step by step through the guide as the stages in developing the research and writing process are built one upon the other.

One of the secrets of success in school is active participation in your learning. Do not be a passive bystander waiting for the teacher to motivate you. Get involved from the first stage of your research and writing assignments and develop a momentum that will get you through the most difficult terrain.

2 REPORTS

A report is informative and factual and does not present an argument or point of view. Reports usually explain or describe something or are biographical. For example, a report might explain weather patterns in a mountainous region, or describe the hunting methods of a specific Native group, or detail the life of a politician.

You need to understand the requirements of the project from the start. If you are unsure of anything, check with your teacher. You should know answers to the following questions:

- Should it be a written or oral report?
- What kinds of sources should be used?
- How should the sources be acknowledged and listed?
- How long should the report be?
- When is it due? What are the penalties for being late?
- Will there be class time to work on the report?
- How will it be marked?
- Should illustrations be used?
- Should a written report be typed or handwritten?

RESEARCH

Selecting the Topic

In most cases, your teacher will decide on a general topic or provide a list of topics from which you can choose. For instance, your teacher may assign the Great Lakes as a topic for a research report. We will use this topic as our example to illustrate the process of researching and presenting a report.

Once you know when the project is due, start planning your time to complete the different stages of the project. These stages are explained in the pages ahead. You should allow about one-third of the time for the preliminary work, one-third for recording the information, and another third for revising, editing, and preparing the final copy. Do not leave the project until the last minute. You will produce a better report if you do not have to rush to meet the deadline.

A "route map" for the research stage of the journey is shown here to guide you.

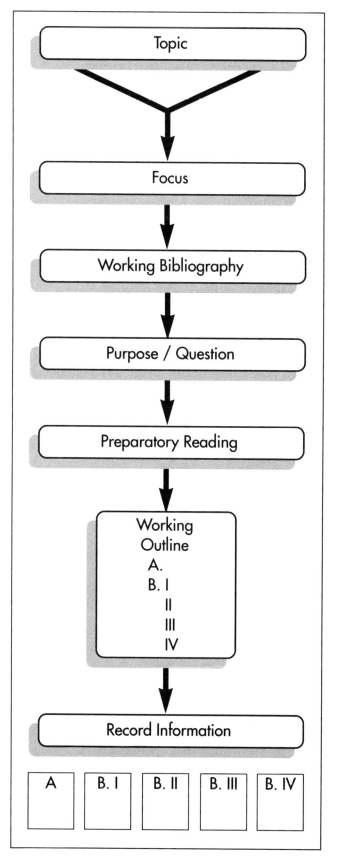

Narrowing the Focus

The Great Lakes is too broad a topic to investigate for an independent research project. Either your final report would be much too long, or you would not be able to cover any points in detail. Suppose you were planning a short trip to the arctic islands. You would have to narrow your visit to one island, such as Baffin Island. Even Baffin Island would be too big to explore in detail on a short trip. After reading about Baffin Island, you might decide to devote your visit to exploring Auyuittuq National Park in depth. In the same way, you would have to narrow the topic for a research project like the Great Lakes. Then you could focus on an aspect or feature that could be investigated in depth.

The best way to narrow your topic is to read and think about it. Textbooks, encyclopedias, and atlases are useful for this exploratory reading.[1] You could also ask your teacher and your librarian for other sources. As you read, try to find the major features of your topic and jot them down in a notebook. A notebook is a good place to keep all your ideas and questions for your project.

Another way to expand your list of features is to form a group with other students and brainstorm the topic. Brainstorming is an exciting process of generating ideas and finding features about a topic. It is both fun and helpful. List these ideas in your notebook as well.

Dozens of different features about the Great Lakes should emerge from a brainstorming session. The following are some possibilities:

- Glaciation
- Birds
- Pollution
- Hydro-electricity
- Welland Canal
- Shipping

- Shipwrecks
- Zebra mussels
- Fishing
- Recreation
- Climate
- Niagara Falls

You can also use a technique called "mapping" or "webbing" to brainstorm ideas and features. One member of the group can use the chalkboard and start with the topic (The Great Lakes) in the centre. Other students can suggest ideas and subtopics that can then be broken down into still smaller units. Notice how a major feature such as pollution can be subdivided.

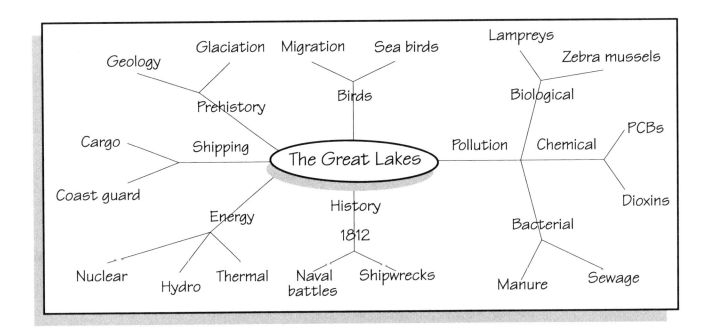

Write as many features as you can in your notebook. The longer the list, the better your chances are of finding one that appeals to you. Next, select those features that interest you the most and then choose just one for your focus. Select a feature that you can handle comfortably. A project on pollution in the Great Lakes might produce too general a report without any real depth. A feature that is too small is also not suitable. For example, narrowing birds to a single species such as an obscure bird like the jaeger would be difficult unless you were an expert bird watcher.

Think carefully before you make your choice. Discuss it with your classmates and your teacher. **Narrowing the topic is very important because the feature that you select will provide the focus for your research.**

After carefully considering the list of features in your notebook, you might first choose pollution. Because this topic is so broad you would discover that there are different forms such as biological, chemical, and bacterial. You might decide to focus on biological and narrow it further to the zebra mussel invasion of the Great Lakes. By isolating the zebra mussel problem, you would be placing a spotlight on it like an actor on a stage. It is clearly illuminated in the bright shaft of light. All attention is on the zebra mussel problem.

It is a good idea to have one or two backup features listed in your notebook in case you run into difficulties with your first choice. For example, you might jot down "chemical contamination" of the Great Lakes and "glaciation" as backup features in case you cannot find information on the zebra mussel problem.

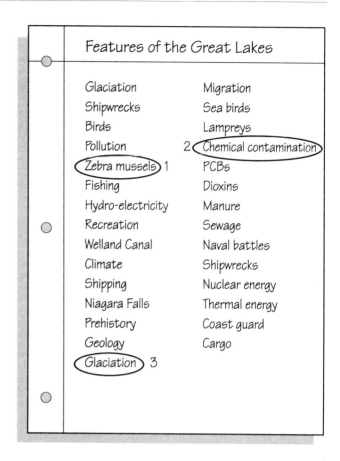

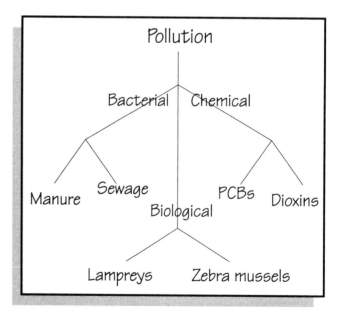

Locating Sources

Your decision to focus on a certain feature gives direction to your project. Your next step is to compile a list of sources of information. If there are not enough sources for your first choice, you may have to use your second choice. Most of your research will probably be done in your community library. There are resources available to you in most libraries that will speed up your search for sources. It is important that you become familiar with the library so that you can make the most use of it. Remember that librarians are always willing to help you.

- The catalogue lists most of the sources held in a library and therefore it is usually the best place to start your search. Many libraries are replacing their card catalogues with computer terminals.

- Periodical indexes are helpful research tools because they enable you to locate articles in hundreds of magazines and academic journals. The following indexes are especially useful for research projects: *Canadian Periodical Index, Readers' Guide to Periodical Literature,* and *Social Sciences Index.* Some journals also publish their own specialized indexes such as *National Geographic Index, 1888–1988* and *Scientific American: Cumulative Index, 1978–1988.* Some libraries may not have these indexes.

- Newspapers are a valuable source of information. Like magazines and journals, there are indexes that will give you quick access to newspaper articles. Some include a number of newspapers such as the *Canadian Index,* while others cover just one newspaper such as *The New York Times Index.*

- Vertical files containing newspaper clippings and pamphlets are kept in many libraries. These files are usually catalogued and contain valuable current information.

- Browsing is an effective way of expanding your list of sources. Locate your "browsing area" in the library by using the catalogue to determine which shelves hold books on your subject. Then check the table of contents and indexes in books about your broad topic. You will often find useful information in these books that would not show up in a catalogue search. The reference section in the library is an especially useful area for browsing. You will find a wide assortment of reference publications such as encyclopedias, atlases, yearbooks, and dictionaries.

- There are probably experts in your community whom you might interview for your project. You should also consider compiling a list of resources in your community such as museums, art galleries, and libraries.

- Talk to your teachers, librarians, and classmates. They will often be able to provide you with useful leads for sources.

As you search for sources, you will be looking for information on your chosen feature. Using a variety of sources can improve a project. To increase the variety of your sources, you might set them out on three separate pages of notepaper headed "Books," "Periodicals," and "General." The periodicals category is for articles in magazines and journals. The general category is for all sources other than books and periodicals, such as films, videos, newspaper articles, photographs, atlases, statistics, graphs, and interviews. As you discover sources, list them under the appropriate heading as shown on this page.

This list of sources is known as your Working Bibliography. Make sure you record the author, title, publication, city, publisher, date, and page number because you will need these details for compiling your final bibliography.

Continue listing all your sources in the manner shown on this page. The code is a shortened form of the title you develop to identify the source during the research. For example, AI stands for "Alien Invasion" and ES stands for *Exotic Species and the Shipping Industry*.

Working Bibliography

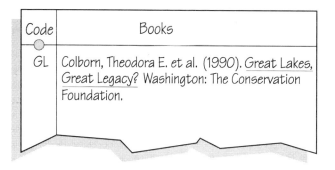

Code	Books
GL	Colborn, Theodora E. et al. (1990). <u>Great Lakes, Great Legacy?</u> Washington: The Conservation Foundation.

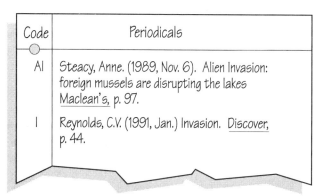

Code	Periodicals
AI	Steacy, Anne. (1989, Nov. 6). Alien Invasion: foreign mussels are disrupting the lakes <u>Maclean's</u>, p. 97.
I	Reynolds, C.V. (1991, Jan.) Invasion. <u>Discover</u>, p. 44.

Code	General
BLI	Beware a lake' s intruders. (1992, October 23). <u>The Globe and Mail,</u> p. A10.
CS	Coming Soon to Area Lakes. (1992, March 1) <u>The Ottawa Citizen,</u> p. E1.
ES	International Joint Commission and the Great Lakes Fishery Commission (1990, September) <u>Exotic Species and the Shipping Industry: Great Lakes – St. Lawrence Ecosystem at Risk.</u>

At this stage, you are just listing the sources. There is no need to sign out the material unless you are concerned that other students will take out all the books on your feature. You should ask your teacher how many sources you should use. If your teacher does not specify the number of sources required, try to list ten spread over the three categories (books, periodicals, general) in your Working Bibliography. Once you think that there are enough sources of information, you are ready to move on to the next phase of the project.

If you are having difficulty discovering sources, you will probably have to change your feature. That is the advantage of having a backup feature ready in your notebook. It is better to change course in the early stages than to discover you have insufficient sources as the deadline gets closer.

It is a good idea to keep your group working together throughout the project. Members of your group can cooperate in developing working bibliographies. If you know what each member is focusing on, you can jot down relevant sources that you come across in your searching. Sharing in this way can expand your list of sources considerably.

Defining the Purpose

The next step is to define more clearly the direction of your research. In other words, what is the precise purpose or objective of your report? You may have developed some ideas while you were building your list of sources.

It may be necessary to read more about the focus of your research to help you decide on the purpose. You can also gather your group and brainstorm possible directions for your project. Write your ideas and questions in your notebook or sketch them in "map" form as shown below.

You may wish to state the purpose as a question such as, "How did the zebra mussels migrate to the Great Lakes?" Or, you may phrase the purpose as a statement: "The purpose of my research is to explain how the zebra mussels migrated to the Great Lakes."

Remember to consider the time assigned for the project. Do not get carried away and pose a question that would produce a book. Also, do not launch yourself on a journey that might be too difficult. Attempting to demonstrate the impact of zebra mussels on algae growth in Lake Erie might be too complex unless you have a good knowledge of science.

Consider carefully the possible directions your report might take and then discuss them with your teacher. After talking to your teacher, you may decide to state your objective as follows: "The purpose of my research is to explain the zebra mussel invasion of the Great Lakes."

You have set your course and you are now ready to embark on the next stage of your journey.

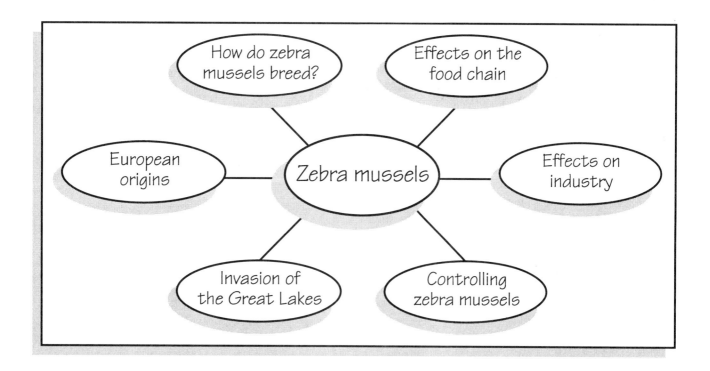

Developing the Working Outline

Once you have established the purpose of your report and you know that enough sources are available, you need to develop a better understanding of the focus of your report. Once again, encyclopedias and textbooks are useful for the preparatory reading. You might also locate and read one or two shorter sources from your list.

A report (or an essay) is like an iceberg—the one-ninth above the water is your final product. But just as all that ice under the water keeps the iceberg floating, a lot of "invisible" work keeps your report above the water. Much of the reading, thinking, brainstorming, and even some of your research notes do not appear in the final copy. All this invisible work provides **a solid foundation for your report.**

In addition to learning more about your feature, the preparatory reading also allows you to start shaping the outline of your report. As you read, keep the purpose of your research in mind. In our example, the purpose is to explain the zebra mussel invasion of the Great Lakes. You are searching for the main sections around which you will build your report.

Jot down your main sections on a separate page headed "Working Outline." List as many sections as you can find, but remember **they must be directly linked to the purpose of your research.** Also, they must be major sections, not specific details. There is no special order to the sections at this stage - just list them as you find them. You will notice that we have listed ten sections in our Working Outline shown on this page.

Working Outline #1

   A. Introduction

   B. Body

      I. Origin
      II. Breeding
      III. Description
      IV. Arrival
      V. Spread
      VI. Effects
      VII. Control
      VIII. Advantages
      IX. Habitat
      X. Food chain

Gather your group to discuss the Working Outlines. Make copies of each member's Working Outline and then brainstorm one another's outlines. This should generate some interesting ideas.

Sometimes after a brainstorming session, you may find your outline has too many sections. Study them carefully. Combine those that are similar and reduce the number of your sections. There is no magic number, but from three to six sections will provide a good working structure. The purpose of your research will determine the number of sections in the outline.

Once you have decided on your Working Outline, review the sections and rearrange them in the best order. If, for example, you were doing a biographical report on Alexander Graham Bell, you might organize the sections in chronological order.

In our zebra mussel example, we listed ten factors in the body of our first Working Outline on the previous page. These were narrowed to four and rearranged in a revised Working Outline shown on this page. The sections were ordered according to time sequence: Origin → Description → Spread → Effects.

Make a copy of your revised Working Outline and take it back to your group for discussion and improvement. You should also discuss your Working Outline with your teacher. This is not the final plan for the report. It is only a starting structure. You may modify it during your detailed research. You may eliminate some sections or you may add more. But the Working Outline does provide a plan that will help shape your report.

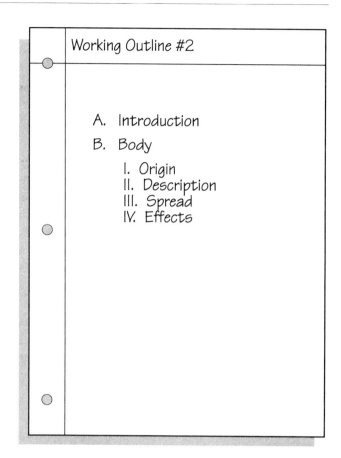

Working Outline #2

A. Introduction
B. Body
　I. Origin
　II. Description
　III. Spread
　IV. Effects

Pause for a moment to look back at the route you have followed:

- You chose a general topic.
- You narrowed it and selected one feature as the focus of your report.
- You compiled a list of sources.
- You defined the purpose of your report.
- You read about the focus of your report.
- You started developing an outline for your report.

Recording Information

Now you are ready to find and record the information you need to prepare your report.

It is impossible to remember everything you read. You need a method for recording and organizing your information. One of the advantages of having a Working Outline is that it provides a structure for your research notes.

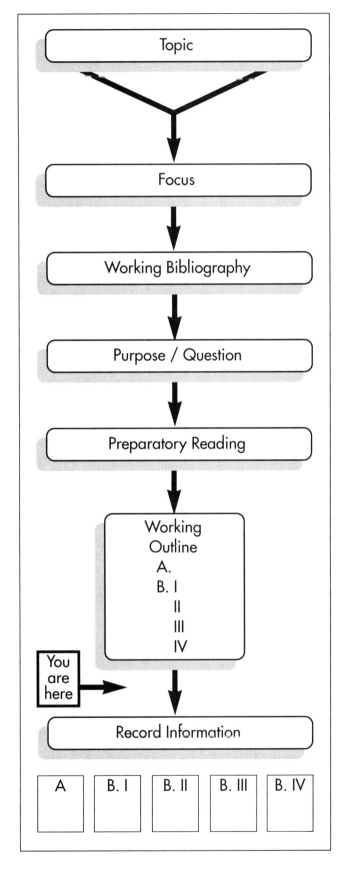

Write the sections of your Working Outline on separate pages of notepaper. Here are the pages set up for recording information on the invasion of the zebra mussels.

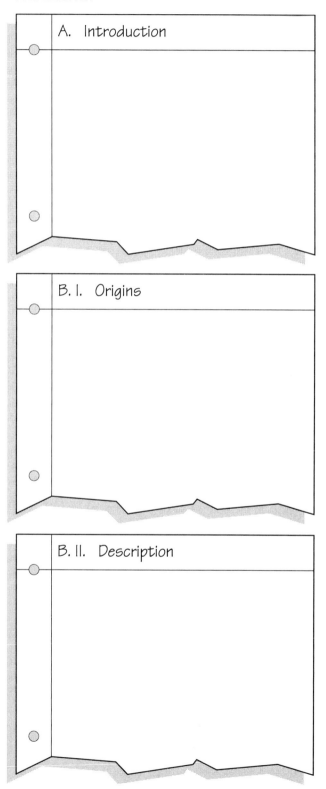

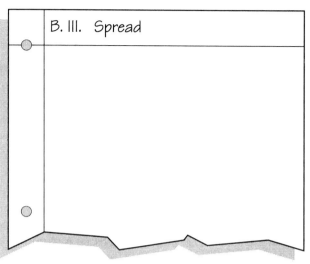

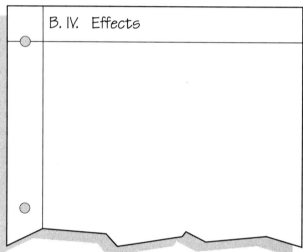

Next, you have to track down your sources. If you have difficulty locating some of the sources on your list, ask your librarian for assistance. Do not panic if you cannot find all the sources in your Working Bibliography. That is why you originally listed more than you really needed. You should be able to complete your report with five or six sources.

Your research system is set up and ready to go. Take one of your sources and start reading, looking for information on the focus of your report. For example, if you were using the article "Alien Invasion" in *Maclean's* magazine, you would discover on page 97 that zebra mussels were first discovered by University of Windsor students. You would write the note briefly **in your own words** on the page headed "Spread." You should mark the source of each note. This is easily done by coding your sources. For example, "Alien Invasion" becomes AI. You should also write down the page reference for the note. Therefore AI 97 indicates that the information is from page 97 of the article "Alien Invasion."

You would continue reading the *Maclean's* article looking for information specifically on the zebra mussel invasion of the Great Lakes (the purpose of your report). On page 98, you would find reference to damage caused by the mussels. You would write the note in your own words on the page headed "Effects," noting the source as AI 98.

This is how the research system works:

- Find relevant information.
- Record it in note form under the appropriate section of the Working Outline.
- Include the source code and page number.

Once you complete source AI, you would work your way through your other sources recording information as explained. Try to use at least three different sources for your information. If you use only one source, it may be biased or unbalanced, or even erroneous. By relying on at least three different authorities, you can get a wider range of views and information.

Collecting information and ideas is a very important stage in preparing your report. You should allow **at least one-third** of the time your teacher has assigned to the project. Try to collect as much information as possible. It will help you produce a better report.

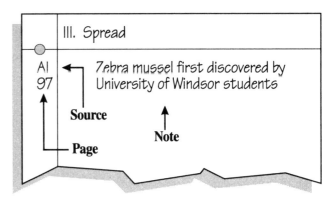

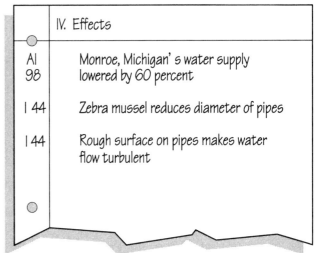

Keep these points in mind when you are recording your information:

- Summarize the information in your own words.
- Be concise, clear, and accurate in your notes.
- The information in your notes must be relevant to the purpose of your report.
- If a piece of information does not fit one of the sections, you have to either create another major section or discard the information as irrelevant to your report.

PRESENTATION

Now that the research stage has been completed, you can start composing your report. Try to present the contents of your report to your readers in the clearest way possible. Your writing skills, combined with the structure you use, will influence how clear your report is.

Shaping the structure of your report is your first task, regardless of whether it will be presented orally or in written form. The ABC formula below is a simple and effective model for structuring reports and essays.

A. Introduction
B. Body
   I.   *Your*
   II. *Main*
   III. *Sections*
C. Concluding Summary

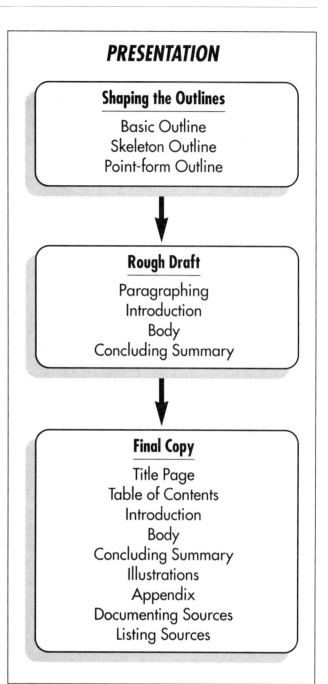

PRESENTATION

Shaping the Outlines

Basic Outline
Skeleton Outline
Point-form Outline

Rough Draft

Paragraphing
Introduction
Body
Concluding Summary

Final Copy

Title Page
Table of Contents
Introduction
Body
Concluding Summary
Illustrations
Appendix
Documenting Sources
Listing Sources

Shaping the Outlines

Once you have finished your research, your notes will be grouped on separate pages according to the sections of your Working Outline. It is difficult to write your final report directly from your notes. A series of stages will help you produce a first-rate report.

Basic Outline

The first stage involves just a name change. Once the research is finished, the Working Outline becomes the Basic Outline as shown on this page. It is possible some sections may have changed during the course of the research. You will notice that one section of our Working Outline (B. I. Origin) was eliminated because of insufficient information. This also required changing the numbers of the main sections. The basic structure of your report is now in place. The Introduction and Concluding Summary will be explained later.

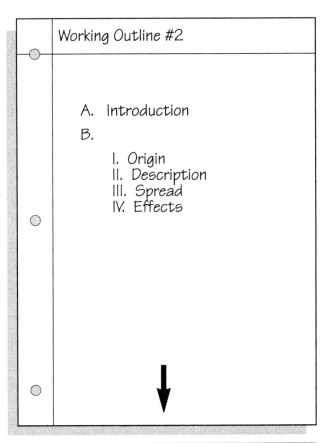

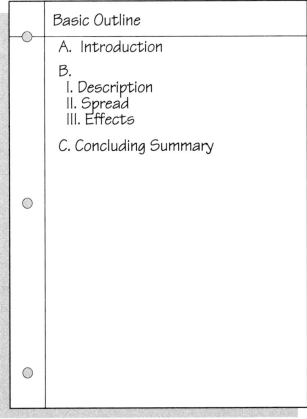

Skeleton Outline

The advantage of having your notes separated on pages according to the structure of your Basic Outline will now become clear. The Basic Outline provides the structure for your report. Each section will have a substructure of its own. The next step is to go through the notes of each section carefully looking for all the important subsections around which you can build the section. Notice how B. II. Spread below has been broken down into three subsections:

1. Across Europe
2. To North America
3. Great Lakes

This stage, containing the main sections and the subsection headings, is called the Skeleton Outline.

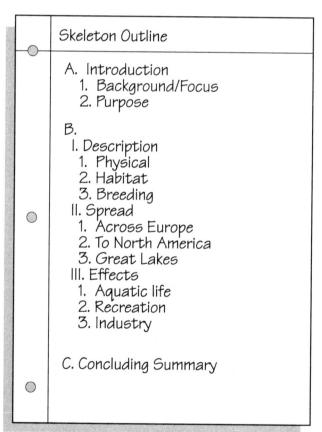

Point-form Outline

Finally, return to your research notes to look for the details that will support each section of the Skeleton Outline. This stage is known as the Point-form Outline. As you read through your notes, **select just the essential information necessary to support your main points.** By trying to cram every note into your report, you could destroy its clarity with irrelevant information. Use as few words as possible when compiling your Point-form Outline. You can always refer to your notes for additional details.

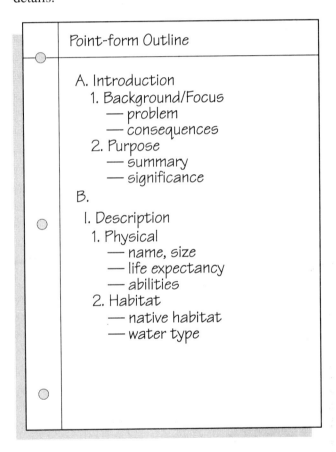

Point-form Outline

A. Introduction
   1. Background/Focus
      — problem
      — consequences
   2. Purpose
      — summary
      — significance
B.
   I. Description
      1. Physical
         — name, size
         — life expectancy
         — abilities
      2. Habitat
         — native habitat
         — water type

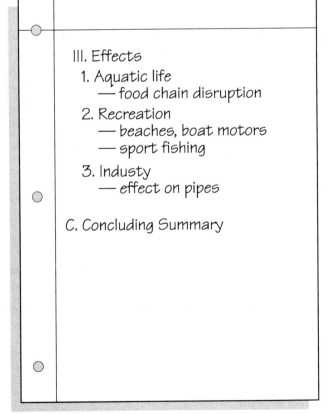

      3. Breeding
         — rate, larvae
         — sex change
   II. Spread
      1. Across Europe
         — isolation
         — clean-up
      2. To North America
         — ballast
      3. Great Lakes
         — habitat
         — travel
         — discovery
         — growth

   III. Effects
      1. Aquatic life
         — food chain disruption
      2. Recreation
         — beaches, boat motors
         — sport fishing
      3. Industy
         — effect on pipes

C. Concluding Summary

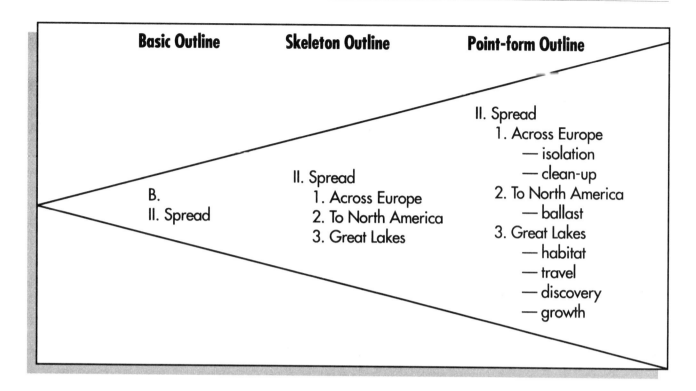

Basic Outline	Skeleton Outline	Point-form Outline

B.
II. Spread
	II. Spread
	  1. Across Europe
	  2. To North America
	  3. Great Lakes
		II. Spread
		  1. Across Europe
		    — isolation
		    — clean-up
		  2. To North America
		    — ballast
		  3. Great Lakes
		    — habitat
		    — travel
		    — discovery
		    — growth

Notice how in the diagram above we have taken section B. II. Spread and demonstrated its expansion at each outline stage. Developing your outlines is not difficult, nor does it take long. The reward lies in having a structure that makes the next step, the paragraphing and the drafting process, easier.

Rough Draft

Paragraphing

One of the advantages of your detailed outlines is that you have a formula for developing your paragraphs. Your paragraphs reflect the structure of your report. Remember that structure is a key component of clarity.

Point-form Outline
B. II. Spread　　　(introductory paragraph)
1. Across Europe　　　(paragraph) 　　— isolation 　　— clean-up
2. To North America　　　(paragraph) 　　— ballast
3. Great Lakes　　　(paragraph) 　　— habitat 　　— travel 　　— discovery 　　— growth
(concluding paragraph)

In this example, we have taken B. II. Spread from the previous page to show how the subsections of the Skeleton Outline provide the paragraph structure. The Point-form Outline provides the supporting details for each paragraph.

Spread

Less than a decade ago, few people in North America could describe a zebra mussel. At that time, it was unheard of outside of Europe. However, as soon as a few arrived in North America, a population explosion began.

For centuries, the zebra mussel could only be found in certain bodies of water in Europe. The rest of Europe, especially the harbours, were too polluted for the mussel. However, with the environmental clean-up of European harbours, the mussels could survive throughout Europe.

It was in a European harbour that the zebra mussel started its journey to North America. It is thought that around 1986, when a transatlantic freighter exchanged its ballast in a European harbour, mussels found their way aboard. When the ship arrived in North America, it dumped its ballast into Lake St. Clair north of Detroit. With it, a group of zebra mussels was set free into completely new territory.

North America was an ideal habitat for the zebra mussel. The water was warm, there were shallow, rocky areas, and the water was less polluted than in Europe. The zebra mussels spread quickly throughout the Great Lakes. Their ability to attach themselves to the hulls of ships and boats sped up the spreading process. The mussels were first discovered in North America in June 1988 by University of Windsor students. By 1991, over a million larvae were to be found in every cubic metre of water in Lake Erie. The zebra mussels had firmly established themselves in the Great Lakes.

The zebra mussel invasion of the Great Lakes was quick. Having spread to European harbours, the zebra mussel simply had to be carried to North America, where it spread with amazing speed.

Topic Sentence ➡

Concluding Sentence ➡

North America was an ideal habitat for the zebra mussel. The water was warm, there were shallow, rocky areas, and the water was less polluted than in Europe. **The zebra mussels spread quickly throughout the Great Lakes.** Their ability to attach themselves to the hulls of ships and boats sped up the spreading process. The mussels were first discovered in North America in June 1988 by University of Windsor students. By 1991, over a million larvae were to be found in every cubic metre of water in Lake Erie. **The zebra mussels had firmly established themselves in the Great Lakes.**

A paragraph is a series of sentences addressing one major idea or step in the development of a report. A topic sentence clearly states the main idea of the paragraph. The topic sentence could be the first sentence or it could be in the middle of the paragraph. In our example above, it is placed in the middle of the paragraph: "The zebra mussels spread quickly throughout the Great Lakes." The remaining sentences provide the supporting details for the main point. The concluding sentence sums up the paragraph. In our example, the final sentence reestablishes the main point: "The zebra mussels had firmly established themselves in the Great Lakes."

The "wagon wheel" illustrates the structure of a paragraph. The hub (main idea) is supported by the spokes (supporting details), and the rim (concluding sentence) ties it together. Without sturdy supporting spokes, the wheel will collapse.

With your detailed outline providing a structure for your paragraphs, you can start weaving your report together in your first draft, usually called a rough draft or working draft.

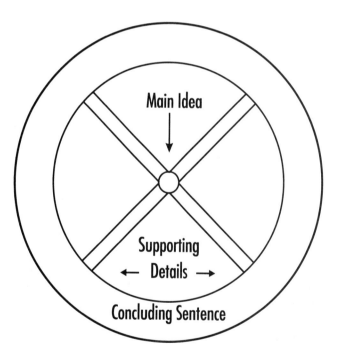

Drafting the Introduction

The Introduction "introduces" your readers to the report. It provides them with interesting background information and it explains the focus of the report. The purpose of the report should be clearly spelled out at the end of the Introduction. Your purpose is a signpost for your reader, indicating the direction of your journey. Do not try to grab the reader's attention by using humour in your Introduction. Your report is a serious piece of work and humour might not set the appropriate tone.

Introductions are usually short, perhaps one or two paragraphs. Your detailed outlines will suggest the paragraph structure for your report. We have shown the Point-form Outline for the Introduction in our example below. We have also shown the Introduction for the zebra mussel report in its final format after careful drafting, revising, and editing.

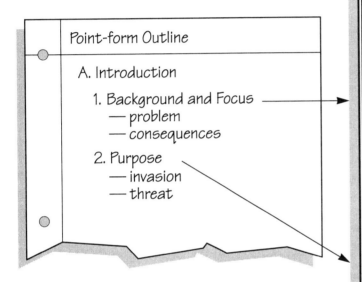

Point-form Outline

A. Introduction

   1. Background and Focus
     — problem
     — consequences

   2. Purpose
     — invasion
     — threat

Introduction

The Great Lakes of North America are important bodies of water to the many people who live on their shores. People rely on the lakes for drinking water, hydro-electric power, fishing, and recreation. All of these areas are being threatened by a new force in the Great Lakes — a mollusk known as the zebra mussel. As a biological pollutant, the zebra mussel has the potential to do great damage to the Great Lakes. In less than 10 years, the invasion of the zebra mussel has created a multibillion dollar headache for the millions who live on the shores of the Great Lakes.

This report will describe the invasion of the zebra mussels and the threat it poses to the Great Lakes ecosystem.

Drafting the Body

The body is the largest and the most important part of the report. This is where you deal with the purpose of your report — where, in our example, we describe the zebra mussel invasion of the Great Lakes.

At this stage, you will have a completed Point-form Outline showing the structure and the supporting details for the body of your report. All the extra effort that went into preparing your detailed outlines will now pay off.

Continue working on your rough draft by expanding the details of the Point-form Outline into sentence and paragraph form. We demonstrated on page 22 how to convert section B. II. Spread of the zebra mussels into paragraphs. We have taken another section of the body, B. III. Effects, to illustrate how it was crafted from the Point-form Outline. It is shown in final form after careful drafting, revising, and editing.

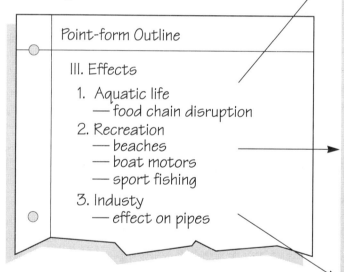

Point-form Outline

III. Effects

1. Aquatic life
   — food chain disruption
2. Recreation
   — beaches
   — boat motors
   — sport fishing
3. Industy
   — effect on pipes

You will notice that the "Effects" section also has an introductory paragraph and a concluding paragraph as we demonstrated on page 22.

Effects

The zebra mussel problem has caught the Great Lakes unprepared. The zebra mussel has had a major impact on the aquatic life, recreational activities, and on industries surrounding the Great Lakes.

The arrival of the zebra mussel in North America created a significant disturbance in the aquatic life of the Great Lakes. The zebra mussel consumes phytoplankton, the base of the lake food chain. This, in turn, jeopardizes the walleye, bass, trout, and perch stocks that normally feed on the phytoplankton. The mussels also infest the spawning beds of others. For example, Lake St. Clair has lost all of its 23 species of clams.

The zebra mussel affects many recreational activities around the lakes, interfering with swimming, boating, and fishing. The mussels infest shallow areas, which also make the best beaches. Their filtering of the water gives it a foul taste. They cling to boats, including the motors, where they can cause serious damage. They cling to fishing gear and transfer diseases to fish. Most importantly for fishers, they have significantly reduced the stock of many sport fish. The zebra mussel has had a serious impact on recreational activities throughout the Great Lakes.

The zebra mussel has done greatest damage to the industries located on the Great Lakes. Because the mussels prefer shallow water, they accumulate in the water intake pipes of many factories and hydro-electric plants. They attach themselves to the insides of the pipes by means of a powerful, gluelike substance. As the zebra mussels multiply, they reduce the diameter of the pipes and eventually clog them completely.

The zebra mussel is a new, disruptive force in the Great Lakes that has created many problems for the residents, and especially, the industries that surround the lakes.

Drafting the Concluding Summary

The Concluding Summary is the part where you weave together your main points and sum up the report. It is not a good practice to add new information to the Concluding Summary. New information at this late stage will confuse your readers. If the information is important, it should be placed in the body, not added as an afterthought to the Concluding Summary.

Although the Concluding Summary is short, usually just one paragraph, it is important. Remember that last impressions are lasting impressions. The Concluding Summary to our example is shown here after careful drafting, revising, and editing.

> **Concluding Summary**
>
> The Great Lakes are threatened by chemical, bacterial, and biological pollution. The recent invasion of the zebra mussels is a dangerous form of pollution that poses serious problems. In the short space of five years, the zebra mussel has had a major impact on the economy and the natural life of the Great Lakes basin. The communities surrounding the Great Lakes will have to develop methods to control the zebra mussels before the damage is irreversible.

Final Copy

Go through your rough draft carefully, checking the structure and eliminating any errors.* Since written expression is so important in developing a clear report, you should read Tips on Style pages 73–74. It is a good idea to work with a partner. You can read each others' drafts, suggesting improvements and correcting errors. Take great care with your final copy because a neat, orderly piece of work will impress the reader. Proofread your report carefully for errors and make sure that it is legibly written or typed.

Subheadings are frequently used in reports but they are not always necessary. Check with your teacher whether you should use subheads. Even without subheads, good paragraphing prevents your readers from getting lost as they read through your report. Also check with your teacher whether your report should be in a folder and if the pages should be stapled.

Title Page

The Title Page should be simple, clear, and neat. Avoid multicoloured title pages with decorative pictures. The following information is normally required on title pages for reports:

- Title
- Student name
- Class/Subject
- Teacher
- Date

Table of Contents

A Table of Contents provides the reader with an outline of the structure of your report. Avoid using the term "body" in your Table of Contents. It was used in the research and the drafting to help you understand the structure of a report. Check with your teacher to determine if a Table of Contents is required.

The Zebra Mussel Invasion of the Great Lakes

Raymond Wade
Geography 1A
Ms. Helen Thexton
January 15, 1993

Table of Contents

A. Introduction
B. I. Description
   II. Spread
   III. Effects
C. Concluding Summary
Appendix
Bibliography

---

* If you would like to know more about revising and editing at this stage, turn to pages 53–54.

Illustrations

Illustrations can be very effective in reports. There are two major types of illustrations: tables and figures. Tables contain columns of statistical data. Figures consist of photographs, maps, drawings, graphs, diagrams, charts, and pictures.

Tables and figures are usually placed at the appropriate spot in the text of the report. If they are lengthy, they can be placed in the Appendix. Select illustrations carefully and do not overwhelm your report with too many pictures, maps, and graphs. Ask yourself whether each table or figure actually illustrates a point in your report.

An example of a graphic illustration is shown below. For advice on developing graphs, charts, and maps and setting up statistical tables, see pages 80–86 of this guide.

Appendix

The Appendix is a useful place at the end of your report for important information that is too lengthy to be placed in the body. For example, you may have a series of graphs and statistical tables about the zebra mussels that, if placed in the body, would disrupt the flow of the report. In that case, they could be placed in the Appendix. In a report on the achievements of Alexander Graham Bell, you may decide to place a time line or chronology of his life in the Appendix. It is important that all material placed in the Appendix is relevant to the report. The Appendix is placed before the Bibliography and each item is numbered and titled. Refer to pages 77–86 of this guide for an example of an Appendix.

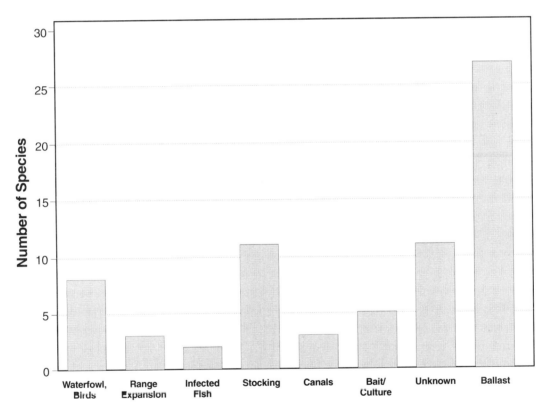

Means of Entry of Foreign Species into the Great Lakes.
Source: International Joint Commission and the Great Lakes Fishery Commission, *Exotic Species and the Shipping Industry: The Great Lakes – St. Lawrence Ecosystem at Risk.* (n.p., September 1990), 24. Reprinted with permission.

Documenting Sources

A common problem in writing reports and essays is using other peoples' ideas and information without acknowledgement. This form of copying is known as plagiarism — it is illegal and unethical. You must identify the sources of important information and give credit to other writers for their ideas. The system of identification often used in reports involves stating the author's name, the date of publication, and the page reference in brackets after the information.*

The reader can then refer to the list of references at the end of the report to obtain the details of the source. This procedure is explained in the next section, "Listing Sources."

> The zebra mussel invasion was unnoticed for some time. The first North American zebra mussels were discovered by University of Windsor students (Steacy, 1989, p. 97). The students were collecting clams on the shores of Lake St. Clair.

You can improve the readability of your report by including the author's name within the sentence and breaking up the reference as shown below.

> One boat hull covered in zebra mussels is enough to begin the infestation of a lake. An Ontario Ministry of Natural Resources fact sheet (1991) asks boaters to leave their boats out of the water for three to five days after being in the Great Lakes (p. 2). This is an effective way to limit the extent of the zebra mussel problem.

*The system for documenting sources and listing sources described on this page is based on the procedures recommended by the American Psychological Association in their *Publication Manual*.

Listing Sources

The brief source references in the report have to be linked to a detailed list of sources. It is common practice to include all sources that proved useful in the preparation of your report. Any one of the following headings may be used:

- References
- List of Sources
- Reference List
- Bibliography
- Works Consulted
- Sources

Sources are listed in alphabetical order by author's surname on a separate page at the end of the report. Do not number your source entries. You grouped your sources "Books," "Periodicals," and "General" in your Working Bibliography to develop a wide-ranging list of sources. Your final bibliography should not be grouped this way — it should be a **single** list of sources as shown below.

Listed on the following page are examples of the more common types of sources.*

Bibliography

Beware a lake's intruders. (1992, October 23). *The Globe and Mail*, p. A10.

Colborn, Theodora E. et al. (1990). *Great lakes, great legacy?* Washington: The Conservation Foundation.

Coming soon to an area lake. (1992, March 1). *The Ottawa Citizen*, p. E1.

International Joint Commission/Great Lakes Fishery Commission. (1990, September). *Exotic species and the shipping industry: The Great Lakes — St. Lawrence ecosystem at risk.*

Reynolds, C.V. (1991, January). Invasion. *Discover*, p. 44.

Steacy, Anne. (1989, November 6). Alien invasion: Foreign mussels are disrupting the lakes. *Maclean's*, p. 97.

Book

ONE AUTHOR

Trigger, B. (1976). *The children of Aataentsic. A history of the Huron people to 1660.* Montreal: McGill-Queen's University Press.

TWO AUTHORS

Strunk, W., Jr., and White, E.B. (1979). *The elements of style* (3rd ed.). New York: Macmillan.

THREE OR MORE AUTHORS

Colborn, T., et al. (1990). *Great lakes, great legacy?* Washington: The Conservation Foundation.

EDITOR

Tarrant, J. (Ed.). (1991). *Farming and food.* New York: Oxford.

NO AUTHOR

It happened in B.C. (1970). Vancouver: BC Centennial '71 Committee.

CORPORATE AUTHOR

International Joint Commission/Great Lakes Fishery Commission. (1990, September). *Exotic species and the shipping industry: The Great Lakes – St. Lawrence ecosystem at risk.*

PAMPHLET

Rothney, G.O. (1964). *Newfoundland: A history.* (Historical Booklet No. 10). Ottawa: Canadian Historical Association.

Magazine

SIGNED ARTICLE

Steacy, A. (1989, November 6). Alien invasion: Foreign mussels are disrupting the lakes. *Maclean's,* p. 97.

UNSIGNED ARTICLE

Passion in Winnipeg. (1992, April 6). *Maclean's,* p. 45.

Encyclopedia

SIGNED ARTICLE

Encyclopedia Americana. (1973 ed.). Hemingway, Ernest, by P. Young.

UNSIGNED ARTICLE

The Canadian Encyclopedia. (1988 ed.). Callwood, June.

Newspaper

SIGNED ARTICLE

von Lowenstern, E. (1990, November 9). English uber alles. *The New York Times,* p. A35.

UNSIGNED ARTICLE

Beware a lake's intruders. (1992, October 23). *The Globe and Mail,* p. A10.

Government Report

National Research Council. (1976). *Climate and food: Climatic fluctuation and U.S. agricultural production.* Washington, DC: National Academy of Sciences.

Interview

Smales, S. (1990, June 5). Personal interview. Toronto.

Film

Costner, K. (Director). (1990). *Dances with wolves.* (Film). New York: TIG and Orion.

Radio and Television Program

Blake, J. (Producer), & Woodruff, J. (Narrator). (1986, May 10). *Apartheid.* (Television). Watertown, NY: PBS.

Map

Physical United States. (Map). (1987). Washington, DC: National Geographic.

Computer Program

PC globe Version 5.0 [Computer program] (1992). Novato, CA: Brøderbund.

(In handwritten or typed reports, titles italicized in this guide would be underlined. Note that only the first word of the title and of the subtitle are capitalized. Proper nouns are also capitalized.)

3 ESSAYS

An essay is a formal piece of writing with a thesis, or point of view, or argument. An essay is not a factual report, a narrative story, or a descriptive composition. An essay allows you to develop your own opinions but requires that you support your opinions or points of view with information and evidence. Unlike the factual report, an essay has your personal imprint in the form of a thesis or argument.

If you are assigned a term paper or research project, check with your teacher whether it is to be an essay or a report.

You should also discuss the following questions with your teacher before starting your essay:

- What kinds of sources should be used?
- How should the sources be acknowledged and listed?
- How long should the essay be?
- When is it due? What are the penalties for being late?
- Will there be class time to work on the essay?
- How will it be marked?
- Should illustrations be used?
- Should the essay be typed or handwritten?

RESEARCH

The research route for the essay is very similar to the course you followed in preparing your report. A route map is provided on this page to guide you.

Selecting the Topic

Sometimes teachers allow students to choose their own essay topics. Always choose a topic that interests you. Let us assume that your teacher has allowed you to choose the topic for your History essay. After careful thought, suppose you selected Native North Americans as the broad subject area you wished to investigate. We will use this topic as our example to illustrate the process of researching and writing an essay.

Discuss your choice of topic with your teacher and clarify the questions listed on the previous page. Start planning your schedule immediately. Remember to allow enough time for the three main phases of the project:

- The preliminary work which includes the stages up to "Gather Sources."
- Recording information.
- Drafting, revising, and preparing the final copy.

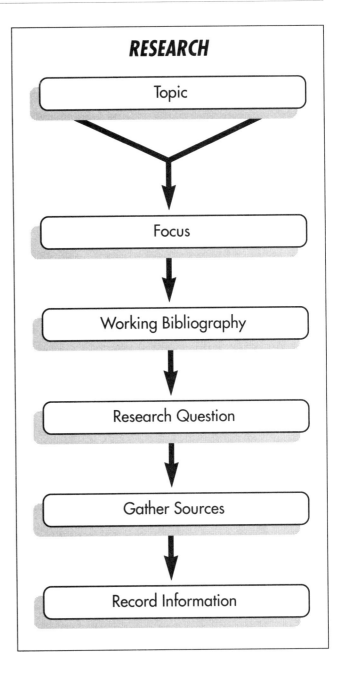

Narrowing the Focus

Native North Americans is a broad topic and, like the Great Lakes topic, it has to be narrowed. In addition to textbooks and encyclopedias, you can use periodical and newspaper indexes for your exploratory reading. If, for example, you look in the *Readers' Guide* under "Indians (Americans)," you will find numerous aspects of Native North American societies listed. Likewise, if you look in the *Canadian Periodical Index* under "Indians of North America," you will find another extensive list. You do not have to read the titles of all the articles. Just look at the section headings. You can check newspaper indexes in the same way. Another approach is to find ideas by looking in the indexes and tables of contents of books such as *Indians of North America* and *The American Indians*. You can generate even more possibilities by viewing films on your topic.

Listed below are just some of the possibilities that may emerge from your exploratory reading:

- Spiritual Values
- Treaties
- Trade
- Political Organization
- Agriculture
- Hunting
- Land
- Reserves
- Nomadic Groups
- Contact with Europeans
- Specific Nations such as the Sioux and the Huron

Gather your group to exchange ideas. Brainstorming ideas in a group is an excellent way to expand your list of issues, ideas, and features. We emphasized the importance of involving your group at every stage of preparing your report. We will not be repeating these suggestions, but it is equally important to discuss and share the progress of your essay with members of your group.

Jot down your ideas and issues in a writing folder or your notebook. We will call it your *Ideas and Questions Journal.* You may want to sketch out a "mapping" diagram (page 6) to show how the different features are related.

Once you have an extensive list of possibilities, circle the ones that interest you the most. Now select

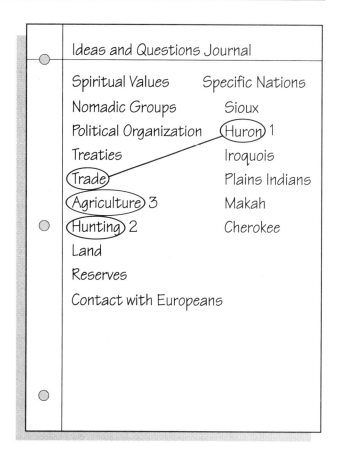

your first choice from this list. We have shown our list of issues and features above. It is important to select an issue that is not so big that you would have too much to write about for the size of your essay. But also be careful to select one that is big enough to find enough information to write about.

After carefully considering the list of issues in your *Ideas and Questions Journal,* you may decide to focus your research on the Huron. Sometimes the narrowing process will involve two or more stages. You may decide that the Huron nation is still too broad a topic to investigate and do further exploratory reading in an encyclopedia. You may then discover that the Huron were prominent traders in their region, and you may decide to focus on their trading system. Discuss your choice with your teacher. Remember, it is a good idea to have one or two backup issues from your short list in case you run into difficulties with your first choice.

Locating Sources

If you used most of the recommended bibliographic aids to complete your report, you are probably a competent researcher. However, it may be worth reading the section on sources again (pages 8–10) to refresh your memory before you start building the Working Bibliography for your essay. In addition to the bibliographic aids mentioned earlier, you may wish to try the following:

- Bibliographies are publications that list books, articles, and other sources on specific topics. They are especially useful because someone has done the searching for you. The following are just a few of numerous bibliographies:

    Bibliographia Canadiana
    International Geographical Bibliography
    Women in American History

- Biographical Indexes provide sources, usually books and articles, on individuals. For example:

    American Women Writers
    Biography Index

- There are a number of publications that provide an analysis of current issues. The back issues provide detailed digests of national and world news and public opinion over the last fifty years.

    Canadian Facts on File
    Facts on File
    Keesing's Contemporary Archives

- There is a wide range of nonprint material available in the form of maps, statistics, photographs, films, taped interviews, videos, television, radio, and computer programs. Ask your librarian for catalogues for these audio-visual sources. Some school libraries also have audio-visual rooms containing equipment such as computers, projectors, laser disc players, and audio and video cassette players. Some libraries have an extensive collection of material on audio and video cassettes and on compact discs.

As you use the bibliographic aids, you will be searching for potential sources of information on your issue. Instead of compiling your Working Bibliography on pages of notepaper, you may want to try index cards this time. One source is entered on each card.

> CA
>
> Trigger, Bruce. The Children of Aataentsic: A History of the Huron People to 1660. Montreal, McGill-Queen's University Press, 1976.

> WHOS
>
> Castellano, Marlene Brant. "Women in Huron and Ojibwa Societies." Canadian Woman Studies 10. 2 (1989): 45–48.

- Continue listing all your sources in this manner.
- The Codes represent key words in the titles and they are used to identify the sources.

You can discover additional sources by searching under terms related to your issue or feature. For instance, if you are exploring folklore among the Inuit do not just look under "folklore" and "Inuit." Consider searching under related headings such as:

- Aboriginals
- religion
- mythology
- traditions
- customs
- legends
- shaman
- spiritualism
- gods
- oral traditions

Computers* are transforming libraries. We have already referred to the banks of computer terminals that are replacing the card catalogue. The on-line computer catalogue, like the card catalogue, only indicates material in the library. It is also possible to search databases in North America and around the world with ease and speed. External database searching is usually known as On-Line Reference. Many libraries offer this service, but there are costs involved.

Increasingly, databases are being put on special computer disks known as CD-ROM. These disks look exactly like audio compact discs, but require a computer with a CD-ROM drive. Many libraries now offer a CD-ROM version of a database which can be searched usually free of charge in the library. Detailed instructions are available with all the above services.

One of the advantages of computerized library services is that you can search for sources using a single key word such as "Huron." The computer will list all works with the word "Huron" in the title.

Using a computer and a modem, you can search library holdings and other databases directly from your computer through a telephone link. You can enter the sources from the screen onto notepaper or cards, or you can have the computer "capture" the information into a file and print it later. If you print out your sources you can cut the printouts and paste the individual sources onto cards or notepaper. Whether or not you use a modem for finding sources, you can use a word processor to list the sources of your Working Bibliography. If you have captured sources using your modem, you can easily route them to the Working Bibliography file.

---

* All computer instructions have been boxed so that you can identify them easily. The computer techniques can be used for all types of research and writing assignments including reports.

You should try to include primary material when searching for your sources. Primary material includes the accounts of eyewitnesses, personal memoirs and recollections, literary works, and official documents. Primary material may be in published form such as an anthology of poems, an autobiography, or a government document such as an international treaty. Primary material is often in unpublished form such as letters and diaries or a taped speech. Original photographs, works of art, and films, as well as archaeological artifacts are also regarded as primary material. You can collect your own primary material by interviewing experts and eyewitnesses, by conducting surveys, and by visiting museums.

Most of your sources will probably be secondary works such as books and articles. Secondary sources are based on primary material. They are written at a later date, and they represent another person's interpretation and explanation of the primary material.

A lot of information is stored in microform. Material in microform includes out-of-print books, government documents, newspapers, periodicals, university theses, pamphlets, indexes, and catalogues. Microfiche (small plastic sheets) and microfilm (on reels) are the two most common microforms. Knowing how to work with microfiche and microfilm readers is an important asset in research and writing today. Ask your librarian to teach you how to use these techniques.

Use your research skills to build a wide-ranging bibliography of sources in which you include books and periodicals, print and nonprint sources, and primary and secondary material. You may run into obstacles and frustrations, but do not give up. Your efforts will be rewarded.

Once you have enough sources of information on your issue, you are ready to move to the next phase. However, if there are insufficient sources despite intensive searching, you will have to select another issue and question from the list in your *Ideas and Questions Journal*. Move fast if you have to change — do not delay.

Defining the Purpose

Like a report, an essay needs direction or purpose. Without it, an essay soon resembles an explorer lost in the woods without a compass. You can give a firm sense of direction to your essay by launching it with a precise and challenging **research question.** This is a crucial stage because the question spells out your purpose. Your task is to answer the question. **The answer will form your thesis, or argument, or point of view.**

Since your purpose is to develop a thesis or argument, you should avoid questions that lead to biographical, narrative, or descriptive answers such as "Who was Sitting Bull?" or "How do the Inuit hunt seals?" Also, do not choose "what if" questions such as "Would the Native Americans have won more battles if they had developed firearms?" This type of question cannot be answered and substantiated by an examination of factual evidence. It is hypothetical and, therefore, inappropriate. "Why" questions such as "Why did war break out in North America in 1812?" are better because they lend themselves to clear, structured answers.

Start then with a concise, challenging question such as "How important was geography in shaping the culture of the Plains Indians?" to give an even clearer focus to your research. If you have difficulty developing a question on your issue, you may wish to do further reading. You should also brainstorm research questions with your group. While you are locating sources for your Working Bibliography, you should list possible questions in your *Ideas and Questions Journal.* Titles of newspaper and periodical articles, for example, will often suggest challenging research questions. Jot down as many questions as possible in your journal and then discuss the most appealing ones with your teacher before making your final decision.

Let us return to our example, the Huron. If our interest is in their trade with the Europeans, we might state our research question as follows: "Why did the Huron become the main fur traders of their region?" With the research question precisely phrased, the direction of the essay is clearly mapped.

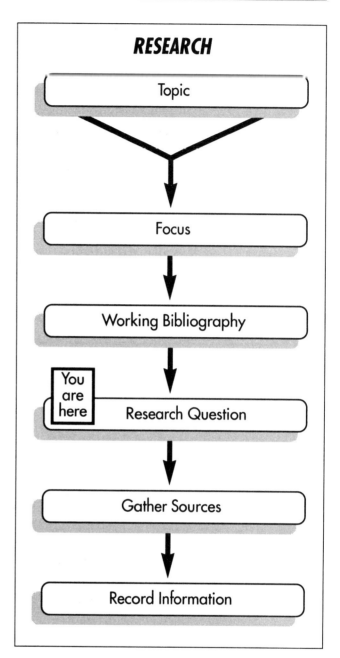

Recording Information

Once you have tracked down and gathered your sources, you are ready to start recording ideas and information. As you find a source, note the library and catalogue number in your Working Bibliography so that you can find it again easily if necessary.

```
CA

Trigger, Bruce. The Children of Aataentsic:
A History of the Huron People to 1660.
Montreal: McGill-Queen's University Press, 1976.

Public Library, Main Branch, 970.3        ✓
```

Remember that your sole task is to develop a thoughtful and convincing answer to your research question. The answer will form your thesis, argument, or point of view.

Since you cannot remember everything you read, a method of recording ideas and information is essential. **You cannot develop a good essay without an organized collection of research notes.** Write your information down so that you do not forget it.

Research involves analyzing, selecting, and recording information and ideas. Analysis means breaking down something into smaller parts. As you read through your material, you examine it carefully extracting important ideas and information (the smaller parts) relevant to your research question. You then record the details in your notes. Try to determine whether a piece of information is established fact or a personal opinion. Remember that **your research question guides your research:** the question directs the analysis, the selection, and the recording of the information. Take special care in the

way you select your notes — to look for information just to "prove" a preconceived position is both unfair and unethical. You should consider all sides of your question and **record all relevant information** whether it supports or contradicts your personal position on the issue that you are investigating.

Recorded notes can take three different forms:

- Summaries of ideas and information.
- Direct quotations.
- Personal ideas, insights, and questions.

You have been introduced to index cards for your Working Bibliography. Try using them for your research notes as well. The smallest index card is most commonly used for recording information.

Index Card Method

If you were doing the Huron essay, you would take one of your available sources, for example, *The Children of Aataentsic* by Bruce Trigger, and start looking specifically for information relevant to the research question. On page 32 there is reference to the high population density of their settlements. Since populous settlements would facilitate trading, you would record the information on an index card.

You must identify the source of the note in case you have to go back to the source for further details. You must also identify the source in case you have to acknowledge it in a reference note. By acknowledging the source, you can avoid charges of illegal copying called plagiarism. There is no need to write out all the publication details (author, title, publisher) again. Simply use the code, which stands for a shortened form of the title. For example, *The Children of Aataentsic* becomes CA as shown on the bibliography card in the previous column. In addition to the source, you must also indicate the page reference for the information. Therefore CA 32 indicates that the information is from page 32 of *The Children of Aataentsic,* as shown in the example on the following page.

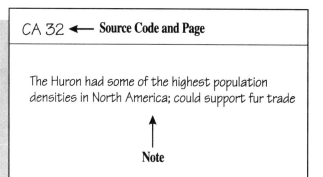

CA 32 ← Source Code and Page

The Huron had some of the highest population densities in North America; could support fur trade

↑

Note

Reflect on what you have done:

- You have discovered relevant information pertaining to the research question.
- You have recorded it in note form.
- You have indicated the source and page number.

Continue reading through the **same** source looking for information relevant to the research question. On page 34, for example, there is reference to agriculture providing most of the food supply. Record the information on an index card and identify the source and page as explained earlier.

CA 34

Crops provided three-quarters of food supply. Freed up males to engage in fur trade.

Once you have completed using source CA, check it off on your Working Bibliography as shown on the previous page and move to your next available source. On page 585 of NAI (*The North American Indians*), for example, you would find a comment on Huron hospitality. You would write down the information verbatim in case it is needed as a quotation. Record it accurately and use quotation marks to indicate that it is a quotation and not a note. The source code, NAI, and the page reference, 585, are recorded as usual.

NAI 585

Jean de Brebeuf commented: "You can lodge where you please, for this nation above all others is exceedingly hospitable towards all sorts of persons, even toward strangers; and you may remain as long as you please, being always well treated according to the fashion of the country."

You would continue reading source NAI recording information on your cards in the manner described. Use the Table of Contents and Index in each book so that you can save time by reading only the relevant pages.

Read all your available sources searching for information relevant to the research question. Continue to systematically record and identify the information on index cards.

Bear these points in mind when you are doing your research on index cards:

- Each card should contain two items:
    1. Source code and page
    2. Note

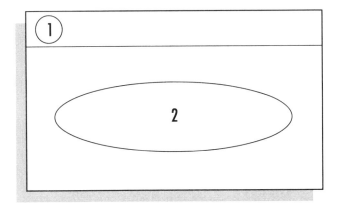

- Write just one note on each card.
- Use the smallest index cards. It is easier to shape your outlines later with small cards.
- Your research cards have no special order, so do not number them. They are all independent, and each is identified by its source code and page reference.
- Finish writing a long note on the reverse side of the card rather than continuing on another card.
- Use cards to copy diagrams, graphs, and statistical tables as well.
- Keep separate "date cards" while researching History essays. Creating a chronology or time line will be easy.
- Record your own ideas either on cards or in your *Ideas and Questions Journal.* Use your initials for the source code.
- Do not confuse bibliography cards, which list sources, with research cards, which contain ideas and information.
- You can use coloured cards to distinguish between different types of cards. For example, you could use white cards for research notes, blue cards for sources, and yellow cards for dates.
- Use a file box or two-ring card folder to organize your cards.

Notepaper Method

Instead of index cards, you can use notepaper to record your information. The methods are similar. If you prefer notepaper to index cards, you should still read pages 38–39 because they contain information not repeated in this section.

You will notice a slight difference between the notepaper method used in the report and this method recommended for the essay. The report notepaper system was based on the structure of the Working Outline, whereas in the essay we have suggested bypassing the Working Outline stage. (Although you may set up a Working Outline and use the same structured notepaper system described in the report section for your essay if you wish. See page 43.)

Rule a 3-cm margin on the right side of the notepaper. Take your first source, *The Children of Aataentsic,* for example, and start looking specifically for information relevant to the research question. As you find relevant information, record it in note form in the centre column. Identify the source by a code and give the page reference in the left margin in exactly the same way described in the index card method. Leave a line between each note and write on one side of the paper only. Nothing is written in the right margin at this stage.

Start a new page for the next source and work your way through it, recording your information. Continue recording information from all your sources as shown in these examples.

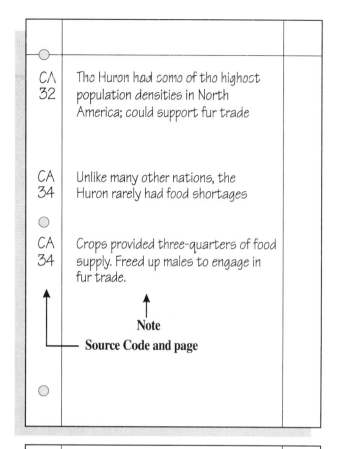

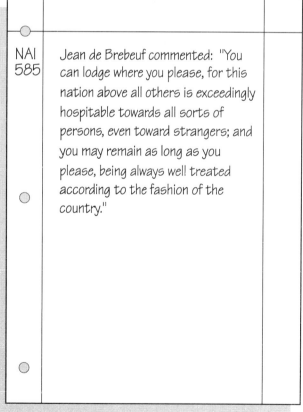

You can also record your ideas and information with a computer. If you prefer the notepaper method, you can set up a word processor file for all your notes. Remember to code each source and give the page reference.

If you prefer index cards, there are many software packages that will let you write, edit, retrieve, and sort cards on the screen. Make sure, however, that your recorded notes can be "exported" to the word processor with which you will write the essay.

Vast amounts of information are being stored on CD-ROM. This information is in a variety of formats such as text, video, sound, graphics, and photographs. For example, the complete works of William Shakespeare are available in "electronic book" format on CD-ROM. You can browse and "import" quotations to your note files directly from CD-ROM sources.

Whatever method you use to record your ideas and information, remember to keep these points in mind:

- Record quotations accurately.
- Summarize ideas and information **in your own words.**
- Be concise, clear, and accurate in your notes.
- Keep adding your own questions and insights to your notes or in your *Ideas and Questions Journal.*
- Make sure your notes are relevant to the research question.
- Be fair; do not select your notes intentionally just to support a particular point of view.
- An extensive and organized collection of notes is essential to preparing a good essay.

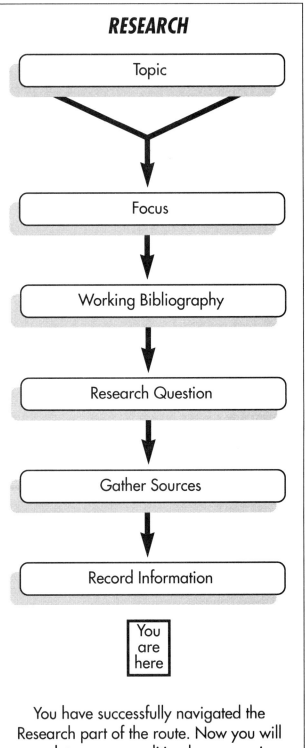

RESEARCH

Topic

Focus

Working Bibliography

Research Question

Gather Sources

Record Information

You are here

You have successfully navigated the Research part of the route. Now you will complete your expedition by composing and packaging your answer.

Some of you may prefer to structure a Working Outline, as described on pages 12-13, before you start recording your information. It is necessary to do the preparatory reading to develop the Working Outline. As you read, keep your research question "Why did the Huron become the main fur traders of their region?" in mind. Jot down the main sections around which you anticipate answering your question. **The research question shapes the contents of the Working Outline.** In our example, the Working Outline would probably look like this:

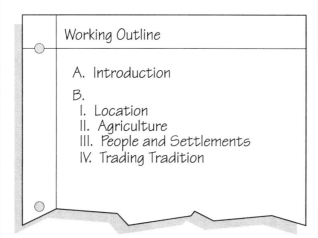

Working Outline

A. Introduction
B.
   I. Location
   II. Agriculture
   III. People and Settlements
   IV. Trading Tradition

If you prefer using notepaper for your research, write the sections of your Working Outline at the top of separate pages as shown on page 15. Then continue to record your information as explained on page 16.

Another method is to use index cards instead of notepaper. We explained how to use index cards **without a Working Outline** on pages 38–40. Read these pages carefully to acquaint yourself with the index card method because we do not repeat the information here. The only difference between the two methods is that **with a Working Outline,** you can assign a section number to each card.

For example, the note card on page 39 would be written as shown below. III refers to section B. III of the Working Outline because the information deals with "Population and Settlements."

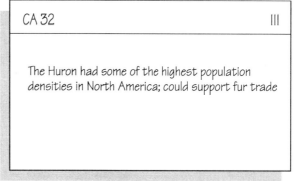

CA 32   III

The Huron had some of the highest population densities in North America; could support fur trade

If you are using index cards **with a Working Outline,** each card will contain three items:
1. Source code and page
2. Note
3. Section heading

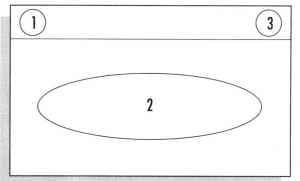

1   3

2

The Working Outline provides a structure for recording information either on notepaper or on index cards. It is not a final plan for the essay because it may change during the research. Your notes (on index cards or notepaper) will be organized in groups saving you time when you start shaping your detailed outlines later.

PRESENTATION

The written presentation of an essay is very similar to that of a report. The main difference is that the message you deliver in an essay is an argument or point of view. The purpose of a report is to inform, explain, or describe. The clarity of your argument greatly depends on the style and structure of your essay. Structure does not suppress creativity; it promotes clear, creative expression.[2] Once again, the ABC formula will provide the structure.

A. Introduction
B. Body
  I.   *Your*
  II. *Main*
  III. *Sections*
C. Concluding Summary

Shaping the Outlines

On completion of your reading and recording, your notes will be on notepaper, index cards, or computer. The next step is to create an outline that will organize your notes*.

Basic Outline

Read through your notes with your question uppermost in your mind. Jot down the main factors around which you can structure your answer. In the example below, we have listed the main factors that will be used to develop an answer to our question: "Why did the Huron become the main fur traders of their region?" This is called the Basic Outline.

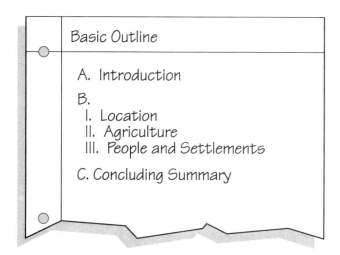

There is no magic number of sections in a Basic Outline — from three to six will handle most questions comfortably. Go through your note cards and arrange them in groups according to the Basic Outline. If you used notepaper for recording your information, separate the individual notes with scissors (that is why you wrote on one side only) and group them according to the Basic Outline.

The next step is to number the cards or notepaper strips according to the section of the Basic Outline into which they fall. Use the upper right-hand corner of the cards or the right-hand column of the notepaper strips for the numbers. For instance, all cards or strips dealing with People and Settlements are labeled III.

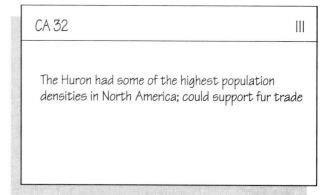

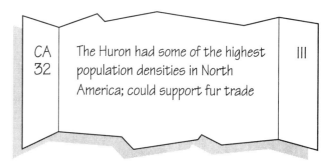

Some notes will not fit into the major sections, and you will have to put them aside. Do not worry if you have an extensive collection of notes and cannot use all of them. To try and force all your notes into your essay would destroy its clarity. The rejected notes are not wasted; they are part of the "invisible foundations" that will support your essay.

---

* If you used a Working Outline for your research, your notes will already be organized. Arrange the Basic Outline as explained on page 18.

If you used a computer to record your material, you might find it easier at this stage to print copies of your notes and organize them manually. But if you do not feel this is necessary, you can reorganize your electronic notes according to your outline. If you used specific index card software, it is easy to group your notes in this manner. If you used a word processor, you can create separate files for each section of the outline and transfer the notes to the appropriate files.

Skeleton Outline

A. Introduction
   1. Background
   2. Focus
   3. Question
   4. Thesis

B. I. Location
   1. Trade with north
   2. Trade with French
  II. Agriculture
   1. Surplus and trade
   2. Men freed up
  III. People and Settlements
   1. Hospitality
   2. Reliability
   3. Density

C. Concluding Summary

Skeleton Outline

Your notes are all grouped and numbered according to the sections of the Basic Outline. Each major section will have its own substructure. The advantage of index cards or notepaper strips is that you can take a section at a time and spread the cards or strips on a table. It is easy to move them around and map out the substructure. This stage is called the Skeleton Outline.

Remember that the purpose of your essay is to develop an answer to your research question and to present it in the form of an argument or thesis. Ask yourself whether each subsection of your Skeleton Outline is directly relevant to the point of view you are developing.

Most word processing programs have an Outline function built in. This function makes it easy for you to create outlines. It will automatically number the sections and subsections as you go along.

If you have been using a computer, look through your electronic notes for the subsections that will make up the Skeleton Outline. If you are using index card software, you may be able to arrange many cards on the screen at once, allowing you to skim them for substructure.

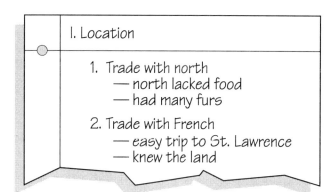

I. Location

1. Trade with north
— north lacked food
— had many furs
2. Trade with French
— easy trip to St. Lawrence
— knew the land

Point-form Outline

Return to your research notes to search for the relevant information and ideas to support your argument. Since not all your notes will be useful, you will have to select only the important information. Use as few words as possible in your Point-form Outline. You can refer back to your notes for additional details if necessary. Since the order of the sections in your outline may change as you prepare your final copy, it is a good idea to use a separate page for each major section in the Point-form Outline.

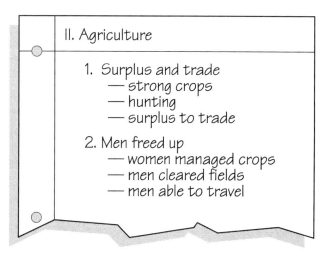

II. Agriculture

1. Surplus and trade
— strong crops
— hunting
— surplus to trade
2. Men freed up
— women managed crops
— men cleared fields
— men able to travel

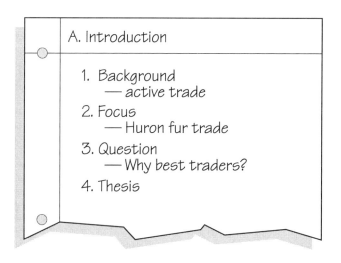

A. Introduction

1. Background
— active trade
2. Focus
— Huron fur trade
3. Question
— Why best traders?
4. Thesis

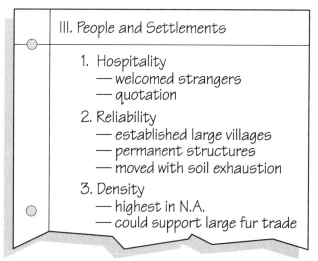

III. People and Settlements

1. Hospitality
— welcomed strangers
— quotation
2. Reliability
— established large villages
— permanent structures
— moved with soil exhaustion
3. Density
— highest in N.A.
— could support large fur trade

The Rough Draft

If you organized the sections of your Point-form Outline on separate pages, it is easy to arrange them in order from least to most important. By finishing with your most important points you give added effect to your argument. Some teachers may prefer a different sequence of sections. Consult with your teacher before you begin your rough draft.

Once you have ordered your Point-form Outline on separate pages, the shape of your essay will start to emerge. You are now ready to put it together. All the work that went into the outlines will pay off. Do not attempt to write your final copy straight from the Point-form Outline. Preparing a rough draft first will help you produce a better essay.

The clarity of your argument is largely dependent on structure and style. The Point-form Outline supplies the structure. It also provides a formula for your paragraphs as we demonstrated in the report (page 22). Since language is so important in developing your argument, it may be a good idea to read Tips on Style (pages 73–74) before you start to write your first draft.

Subheads tend to break up the flow of an essay and you should avoid using them. Careful paragraphing eliminates the need for subheads, because topic sentences provide the signposts that will guide your readers through the essay.

How long should the essay be? This is one of the most common questions raised by students. Your teacher will usually set a word limit for essays. If no limit is set, keep your essays concise and compact. Above all, make sure that you answer your research question.

Since you may be using quoted material in your essay, you should read the section on Quotations (page 56) before starting your draft. In addition, you need to know how to acknowledge the quotations as well as other writer's ideas. Therefore, you should also read the section on documenting your sources (pages 57–58) before writing your draft.

Drafting the Introduction

The Introduction is short but important because first impressions influence a reader. Introductions will vary in length between 10 percent and 20 percent of the overall length of the essay. The length will be determined by the nature of the essay — a controversial issue will probably need a longer introduction — or by the preference of your teacher.

The funnel diagram opposite offers an effective structure for an Introduction for a rescarch essay.[3] First you provide the **background** information that your reader needs to know about the topic. Next explain the **focus** of your assignment. Then you should indicate the **purpose** of your essay — to provide the reader with a signpost showing the direction of your project. Stating your research question is probably the clearest means of expressing the purpose of your essay.

Finally, state your **thesis** or argument clearly. Your **thesis statement** is your answer to the research question summed up in one or two sentences. It is important to inform your readers of your position or point of view *before* you start developing the body of your essay.

Another advantage of the funnel formula is that it provides a structure for paragraphing your introduction. You do not have to follow this structure precisely — modify it to your liking.

You will find the Introduction to the Huron essay on this page. It is shown here in its final format after drafting, revising, and editing. You will notice that it follows quite closely the structure of the funnel formula. Discuss the Introduction with your teacher, because teachers differ over the contents of an Introduction. For example, some teachers like the use of the pronoun "I" in the thesis statement; others discourage it.

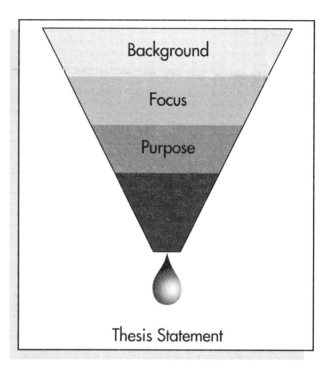

Thesis Statement

In the seventeenth century, there was an active fur trade between the Natives of North America and the Europeans. From 1616 to 1649, the Huron were the central traders in a large fur trading empire. They were the intermediaries between the Native fur producers of the North and the French. There were many nations in the area, but the Huron were the major traders. This raises an important question: Why were the Huron the main fur traders of their region?

Three factors made the Huron the most successful fur traders. They had a solid agricultural base and they had a favourable location. Also, the French chose to deal with the Huron because they lived in established settlements and welcomed visitors.

Drafting the Body

The body is the most important part of the essay. It is in the body that you will develop and support the thesis that you stated at the end of the Introduction. Remember, you are not offering *proof;* you are offering *support* for your theory. Theories are frequently revised even in the sciences.

You cannot use all the available evidence on your topic, and so you select first from your sources to create your notes. Then you sift through your notes and selected the relevant and significant material to build your outlines. Check carefully that all the ideas and information are closely linked to your argument. Irrelevant details will destroy the focus of your essay and weaken the argument. You must be fair in your choice of material. **Your responsibility is to maintain a balanced and open-minded approach in composing your argument.**

Your outlines, in addition to ensuring structure, also organize your paragraphs. Paragraphs are like links in a chain. One weak link makes the chain weak. Likewise, your essay is only as strong as its paragraphs. We have reproduced one section of the body to demonstrate how the outline provides structure and supporting detail for the paragraphs. Note how the introductory paragraph acts as a transitional paragraph by providing a link with the previous section.

Point-form Outline

B. II. Agriculture (introductory paragraph)

1. Surplus and trade (paragraph)
— strong crops
— hunting
— surplus to trade

2. Men freed up (paragraph)
— women managed crops
— men cleared fields
— men able to travel

(concluding paragraph)

Like their location, the agriculture of the Huron was important in supporting the fur trade. The Huron had an abundant food supply that allowed them to trade food. The Huron also hunted less, and so the men were free to trade.

While other nations relied mostly on hunting and gathering, the Huron obtained three-quarters of their food supply from crops. They farmed corn primarily, but also cultivated squash, tobacco, beans, and sunflowers. The Huron crops were plentiful and reliable. In fact, the hunting that the Huron did was mainly for clothing and tools, not for food. This remarkable food base left the Huron with more food than they needed, while other nations did not have enough. The Huron became food suppliers and traded much of their surplus food to the Native peoples in the north in return for furs.

The Huron women were primarily responsible for their flourishing agriculture, and this allowed the men to leave the villages to trade. The women planted and harvested the crops after the men cleared the fields. Because the Huron were settled, clearing fields had to be done only infrequently. During the summer, the men were free to travel and trade. Historian Diamond Jenness has noted that "as soon as the planting ended...the men scattered in all directions to trade with neighbouring peoples." In nations that relied more upon hunting for their food, the men were occupied with hunting in the summer and unable to trade. The Huron did not face this difficulty.

The agricultural base of the Huron set them apart from others in their region. Less hunting meant more time to trade. They traded their surplus food for furs and then traded the furs to the French.

Drafting the Concluding Summary

The Concluding Summary is short, usually just a paragraph. However, it is important. It is your last chance to convince your readers of the validity of your thesis. In this section you weave together the main reasons supporting the conclusions you developed in the body of the essay.

Sometimes it can be effective to start the Concluding Summary with the research question, since this reminds the reader of the purpose of the essay. For example, the Huron essay could have started with "Why did the Huron become the main fur traders of their region?" Then you could proceed to sum up your argument. Try to be more original than concluding your essay as follows: "In conclusion, I would like to repeat that the Huron became the main fur traders because of their location, their solid agricultural base, and their relationship with the French."

Avoid adding new information in support of your thesis in the concluding paragraph because it will confuse your readers. All important ideas and information should be included in the body. Also, do not insert quotations into the Concluding Summary for dramatic effect.

Like the initial impact of the Introduction, the final impression created by the Concluding Summary is important. The concluding section of the Huron essay is reproduced here as an example. It is shown in its final format after drafting, revising, and editing.

> A combination of factors made the Huron the main fur traders of their region. The Huron were located between the fur producers of the north and the fur consumers of the south, making them natural trading intermediaries. They had many stable crops, so they could support themselves and trade surplus food to others. Their productive agricultural base also allowed the men to travel to trade. The French liked dealing with the Huron because of their hospitality, and the fact that they were settled made them reliable traders. The Huron were able to develop and maintain their large trading network because of these advantages over other nations.

Reflect on what you have done:

- You have shaped the structure of your essay.
- Your outlines provide a formula for organizing your paragraphs.
- You are aware of the importance of a clear, focused development of your thesis in the body.
- You understand the roles of the Introduction and the Concluding Summary.
- You have read about using quotations and acknowledging your sources.

You are now ready to write your first draft. Use double spacing and write legibly. Double spacing will allow you to revise and edit, and legible writing means that you, or someone else, can read the draft aloud.

Most word processors allow you to work on two documents at the same time, usually by splitting the screen into two "windows." Bring up your outline in one window, and then begin writing the essay in the other window. You can flip back and forth easily. You can also bring up the files that serve as your electronic notes in one window, and transfer relevant information from that window into the window where you are writing the draft. See below for an example.

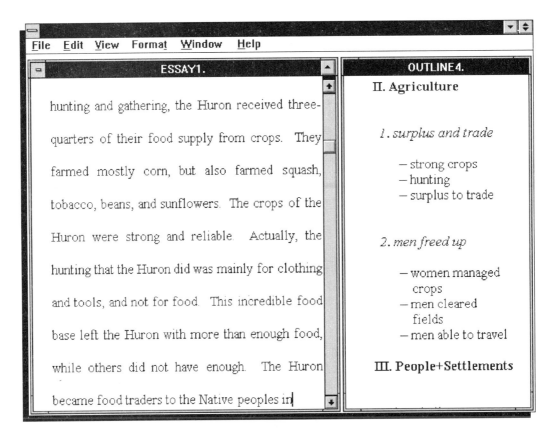

Printed with permission of Microsoft Canada, Inc.

Revising and Editing

Once you have typed or written your draft you are ready to start revising and editing. Revising involves rewriting sections and restructuring paragraphs, while editing is the fine tuning of the revised draft. This is an important stage, and you must allow time in your schedule for revising and editing. It is also a good time to gather your group again to help revise and edit one another's drafts.

If you based your rough draft on a structured outline, your revision time will be reduced. The extra work that went into the preparatory stages invariably pays off in the long run.

Your first task is to examine the order of the main sections of the body. Although you may have rearranged the structure at the Point-form Outline stage, the order might not work well when written out in the rough draft. The question to ask yourself is whether there is a logical flow in the sequence of the sections. Often, one moves from the least to the most important sections, but that sequence is not successful in all essays.

Check the Introduction to make sure that both the purpose and your point of view are clearly spelled out. Does the Concluding Summary serve its purpose?

Once you are satisfied with the overall structure, look closely at the paragraphing. Circle the topic sentence in each paragraph to ensure that there is a central focal point. Is there sufficient supporting detail in each paragraph? Is there a unity to each paragraph? Have you eliminated unnecessary words and phrases? These are the questions you should ask yourself as you revise your draft. But above all, ask yourself whether the essay develops a clear point of view.

The major changes are made at the revision stage. If you have many changes, it may be necessary to rewrite your draft. This is not wasted time because it will improve the quality of the final copy.

The next step is to read your draft aloud. You can read it to yourself or tape-record it. You may read it to your group or to a friend. Perhaps someone else could read it while you listen. If your essay sounds awkward and disjointed, you will have to revise it until it flows smoothly and naturally.

Read Tips on Style pages 73–74 before starting to edit your revised draft. Editing is the fine tuning and polishing of your draft. Read through slowly, checking spelling and grammar carefully. Does your punctuation improve the way your essay reads? Have you chosen your words carefully? Examine your quoting and documenting of sources for accuracy. When you have completed the editing, ask a member of your group to read the draft and suggest improvements. Finally, read it aloud another time. It should now be a polished piece of writing.

The extra time spent in revising and editing is well worth it. You should see a real improvement between your rough draft and your final copy.

The word processor is a valuable editing tool. It can speed up the editing and revising process, and enhance the quality of your writing assignments. The advantage of word processing is that once the information is keyed in, revision and editing can be done without rewriting or retyping the draft.

It is not always easy to get a feel for the overall structure of an essay on a video monitor, nor is it easy to detect punctuation or spelling errors. Many students find it easier to revise and edit on a printed copy of the draft. Another advantage of a hard copy is being able to read it aloud. Members of your group can also read and check it. It is easy to make the changes on the screen and then print out another copy for editing. You should keep all copies in case you need material later that you deleted in earlier versions.

If you are reviewing and editing on the screen, you may want to name each revision, such as "ESSAY1," "ESSAY2," and so on. This will allow you to return to previous revisions for material that you deleted in later versions. After you have submitted your final copy, you can erase the earlier files.

It is important to save your draft frequently to avoid losing the essay if there is a power failure.

If your word processor has a spell check or a grammar check program, take advantage of it before printing the final draft. But remember that you must edit your work carefully even after you have used the software program. Spell checks have no way of knowing that when you wrote "to" you meant to write "too" or "two."

The Final Copy

Leave yourself enough time to set aside your edited draft for a few days before you prepare the final copy. Ask your teacher about the final format for your essay. For example, should it be typed or handwritten, should the pages be stapled, and should it be in a soft or hard folder? Then write it out legibly and proofread it carefully. An error free, neatly packaged essay should be your aim.

Preparing your final copy should be quick and painless if you have used a word processor for writing and editing. The appearance of your essay can be improved by computer technology. Software programs can ensure a clean, professional type and provide a variety of graphic illustrations. Most schools have computer facilities that are accessible to students so there is no need to purchase expensive equipment. Although not all teachers require typed assignments, combining literary ability with typing and computing skills is an important asset today. But remember that it is substance, not technological dazzle, that characterizes a good essay.

It is a good idea to keep a backup copy of your essay in case the original is lost.

Reread the report section on how to lay out your Title Page and Table of Contents (page 27). Normally, you would not put your title in question form. Instead of using your research question for the Huron essay, you could state the title as follows: "The Huron Trading System." Keep the title concise and use a subtitle only if it clarifies the title. If you are using illustrations and an Appendix you should check page 28.

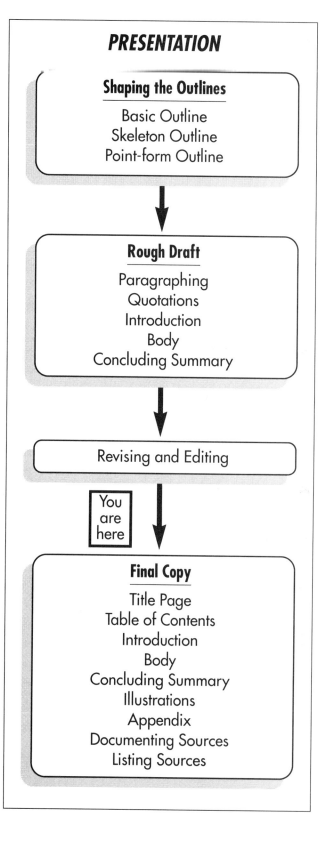

PRESENTATION

Shaping the Outlines
Basic Outline
Skeleton Outline
Point-form Outline

Rough Draft
Paragraphing
Quotations
Introduction
Body
Concluding Summary

Revising and Editing

You are here

Final Copy
Title Page
Table of Contents
Introduction
Body
Concluding Summary
Illustrations
Appendix
Documenting Sources
Listing Sources

Quotations

Carefully selected quotations can be very effective in supporting your arguments. Keep your quotations brief and do not over use them. Do not use quotations just to make your essay longer. You should not only have a good reason for using every quotation, but each quotation should be clearly linked to your thesis.

Short quotations should be included within the text of the essay and placed in double quotation marks. Try to weave the quoted material naturally with your writing.

> Historian Diamond Jenness has noted that "as soon as the planting ended...the men scattered in all directions to trade with neighbouring peoples."

Sometimes you may need to use only part of a quotation. Use three spaced periods (. . .) to indicate that words are missing. This is known as an ellipsis.

Longer quotations of two or more sentences should be separated from the text as shown below. The quoted passage should be indented five spaces from the left margin. It is usually introduced with a colon. Quotation marks are not used. Either double or single spacing may be used.

> Jean de Brebeuf, who had many dealings with the Huron, commented on their hospitality:
>
> > You can lodge where you please, for this nation above all others is exceedingly hospitable towards all sorts of persons, even toward strangers; and you may remain as long as you please, being always well treated according to the fashion of the country.

You must quote your material accurately. You must also acknowledge your quotations carefully to avoid accusations of plagiarism. We have excluded the references for the above quotations to simplify the explanation. The procedures for acknowledging your sources are explained in the next section.

Documenting Sources

Whether you are using direct quotations or paraphrased ideas, you must acknowledge your sources. Providing thc sources of your information gives credit to other writers for their ideas. It also means the information can be checked for accuracy.

You were introduced to the parenthetical (bracketed) procedure in the presentation of a written report (page 29). Another common method of documenting your sources is to use numbered footnotes or endnotes. A number is placed above the line at the end of the sentence or quotation. These reference numbers are numbered consecutively throughout the essay. Each of these numbers has a corresponding entry either at the bottom of the page (footnote) or on a separate page at the end of the essay (endnote). On the following page, we have reproduced a section of the Huron essay to illustrate the use of footnotes. See page 89 of the guide for an example of endnotes.

Listed below are examples of the more common types of reference notes. These examples are based on the procedures in the latest edition of *A Manual for Writers* by Kate Turabian.

Book

ONE AUTHOR

[1] Bruce Trigger, *The Children of Aataentsic: A History of the Huron People to 1660* (Montreal: McGill-Queen's University Press, 1976), 335.

TWO AUTHORS

[2] William Strunk, Jr. and E.B. White, *The Elements of Style,* 3rd ed. (New York: Macmillan, 1979), 15.

THREE OR MORE AUTHORS

[3] Theodora Colborn, et al., *Great Lakes, Great Legacy?* (Washington: The Conservation Foundation, 1990.), 154.

EDITOR

[4] John Tarrant, ed., *Farming and Food.* (New York: Oxford, 1991), 74.

NO AUTHOR

[5] *It Happened in B.C.* (Vancouver: BC Centennial '71 Committee, 1970), 12.

CORPORATE AUTHOR

[6] International Joint Commission and the Great Lakes Fishery Commission, *Exotic Species and the Shipping Industry: The Great Lakes – St. Lawrence Ecosystem at Risk* (n.p., September 1990), 25.

PAMPHLET

[7] G.O. Rothney, *Newfoundland: A History,* Historical Booklet, no. 10 (Ottawa: Canadian Historical Association, 1964), 5.

Magazine

SIGNED ARTICLE

[8] Anne Steacy, "Alien Invasion: Foreign Mussels Are Disrupting the Lakes," *Maclean's,* 6 November 1989, 97.

UNSIGNED ARTICLE

[9] "Passion in Winnipeg," *Maclean's,* 6 April 1992, 45.

Encyclopedia

SIGNED ARTICLE

[10] Philip Young, "Hemingway, Ernest," in *Encyclopedia Americana,* 1973 ed.

UNSIGNED ARTICLE

[11] "Callwood, June," in *The Canadian Encyclopedia,* 1988 ed.

Newspaper

SIGNED ARTICLE

[12] Enno von Lowenstern, "English Uber Alles," *New York Times,* 9 November 1990, A35.

UNSIGNED ARTICLE

[13] "Beware a Lake's Intruders," *The Globe and Mail* (Toronto), 23 October 1992, A10.

GOVERNMENT REPORT

[14] National Research Council, *Climate and Food: Climatic Fluctuation and U.S. Agricultural Production.* (Washington, DC: National Academy of Sciences, 1976), 11.

Interview

[15] Sandra Smales, personal interview, 5 June 1990, Toronto.

Film

[16] Kevin Costner, dir. *Dances with Wolves* (New York: TIG and Orion, 1990).

Radio and Television Program

[17] "Apartheid," narr. Judy Woodruff, prod. John Blake, *Frontline,* PBS, WBNE, Watertown, NY, 10 May 1986.

Map

[18] *Physical United States,* map, (Washington, DC: National Geographic Society, 1987).

Computer Program

[19] PC Globe Version 5.0 (Novato, CA: Brøderbund).

If there is no place of publication given, use n.p.; for no publisher, use n.p.; and if both are missing it is permissible to use only n.p. If no date is provided, insert n.d.

All titles have been italicized in these examples. If you are using a word processor, titles may be boldface or italicized. In handwritten or typed essays, titles italicized in this guide would be underlined.

If you refer to a source that has already been mentioned, there is no need to repeat all the publication details. Just use an abbreviated form containing the author's surname and the page reference.

Example:

[5] Sinclair 99.

Another example is shown in the opposite column.

M̲ost word-processing programs have footnote and endnote features. Consult your software information manual for details.

While other nations relied mostly on hunting and gathering, the Huron obtained three-quarters of their food supply from crops. They farmed corn primarily, but also cultivated squash, tobacco, beans, and sunflowers. The Huron crops were plentiful and reliable.[1] In fact, the hunting that the Huron did was mainly for clothing and tools, not for food.[2] This remarkable food base left the Huron with more food than they needed, while other nations did not have enough. The Huron became food suppliers and traded much of their surplus food to the Native peoples in the north.

The Huron women were primarily responsible for their flourishing agriculture, and this allowed the men to leave the villages to trade. The women planted and harvested the crops after the men cleared the fields. Because the Huron were settled, clearing fields had to be done only infrequently. During the summer, the men were free to travel and trade. Historian Diamond Jenness has noted that "as soon as the planting ended...the men scattered in all directions to trade with neighbouring peoples."[3] In nations that relied more upon hunting for their food, the men were occupied with hunting in the summer and unable to trade. The Huron did not face this difficulty.

---

[1] Diamond Jenness, *The Indians of Canada,* 7th ed. (Toronto: University of Toronto Press, 1977), 202.

[2] Bruce Trigger, *The Children of Aataentsic: A History of the Huron People to 1660.* (Montreal: McGill-Queen's University Press, 1976), 34.

[3] Jenness 113.

Listing Sources

You must compile a list of the information sources you used and attach the list to your essay. Any one of the following headings may be used:

- References
- List of Sources
- Reference List
- Bibliography
- Works Consulted
- Sources

The sources should be listed in alphabetical order by author on a separate page at the end of the essay. If you used index cards for your Working Bibliography, it is easy to rearrange them in alphabetical order.

Note that there are minor differences between the procedures for documenting and listing sources. You will notice for example that the order of the names is different, as well as the indentation. Shown below are examples of listing the more common types of sources. Again, they are based on the procedures described in Kate Turabian's *A Manual for Writers.*

Book

ONE AUTHOR

Trigger, Bruce. *The Children of Aataentsic: A History of the Huron People to 1660.* Montreal: McGill-Queen's University Press, 1976.

TWO AUTHORS

Strunk, William Jr. and E.B. White. *The Elements of Style* 3rd ed. New York: Macmillan, 1979.

THREE OR MORE AUTHORS

Colborn, Theodora et al. *Great Lakes, Great Legacy?* Washington: The Conservation Foundation, 1990.

EDITOR

Tarrant, John, ed. *Farming and Food.* New York: Oxford, 1991.

NO AUTHOR

It Happened in B.C. Vancouver: BC Centennial '71 Committee, 1970.

CORPORATE AUTHOR

International Joint Commission and the Great Lakes Fishery Commission. *Exotic Species and the Shipping Industry: The Great Lakes – St. Lawrence Ecosystem at Risk.* N.p., September 1990.

PAMPHLET

Rothney, G.O. *Newfoundland: A History.* Historical Booklet, no. 10. Ottawa: Canadian Historical Association, 1964.

Magazine

SIGNED ARTICLE

Steacy, Anne. "Alien Invasion: Foreign Mussels Are Disrupting the Lakes." *Maclean's,* 6 November 1989, 97.

UNSIGNED ARTICLE

"Passion in Winnipeg." *Maclean's,* 6 April 1992, 45.

Encyclopedia

SIGNED ARTICLE

Young, Philip. "Hemingway, Ernest." *Encyclopedia Americana.* 1973 ed.

UNSIGNED ARTICLE

"Callwood, June." *The Canadian Encyclopedia.* 1988 ed.

Newspaper

SIGNED ARTICLE

von Lowenstern, Enno. "English Uber Alles." *New York Times,* 9 November 1990, A35.

UNSIGNED ARTICLE

"Beware a Lake's Intruders." *The Globe and Mail* (Toronto), 23 October 1992, A10.

Government Report

National Research Council. *Climate and Food: Climatic Fluctuation and U.S. Agricultural Production.* Washington, DC: National Academy of Sciences, 1976.

Interview

Smales, Sandra. Personal interview. 5 June 1990, Toronto.

Film

Costner, Kevin, dir. *Dances with Wolves*. New York: TIG and Orion, 1990.

Radio and Television Program

"Apartheid." Narr. Judy Woodruff. Prod. John Blake. *Frontline*. PBS, WBNE, Watertown, NY. 10 May 1986.

Map

Physical United States. Map. Washington, DC: National Geographic Society, 1987.

Computer Program

PC Globe Version 5.0. Novato, CA: Brøderbund.

If there is no place of publication given, use N.p.; for no publisher, use n.p.; and if both are missing it is permissible to use only n.p. If no date is provided, insert n.d.

All titles have been italicized in these examples. If you are using a word processor, titles may be boldface or italicized. In handwritten or typed essays, titles italicized in this guide would be underlined.

When listing two or more sources by the same author, enter the second source as shown for Bruce Trigger opposite.

Bibliography

"1491: America Before Columbus." *National Geographic*, October 1991, 2–99.

Castellano, Marlene Brant. "Women in Huron and Ojibwa Societies." *Canadian Woman Studies*, 10.2 (1989): 45–48.

Jenness, Diamond. *The Indians of Canada*, 7th ed. Toronto: University of Toronto Press, 1977.

Owen, Roger et al., eds. *The North American Indians*. New York: Macmillan Company, 1967.

Trigger, Bruce. *The Children of Aataentsic: A History of the Huron People to 1660*. Montreal: McGill-Queen's University Press, 1976.

_____. *The Impact of the Europeans on Huronia*. Vancouver: Copp Clark Publishing, 1969.

4 COMPARATIVE ESSAYS

Comparative essay questions are common in examinations and are also frequently set as prepared questions for in-class tests or as take-home examinations. Short comparative essays not requiring extensive research and documentation of sources are also common. However, comparative assignments are not usually set as major research projects until senior high school.

Comparing and contrasting can be more difficult than writing the single focus report or essay that we have described in this guide. In a comparative assignment, you have to **show the connection or relationship** between two individuals, events, or ideas. You are not just describing them; you are comparing them and focusing on their similarities and/or differences.

For example, in English you may be asked to compare two characters in a novel. In Geography, you may have to compare fishing methods on the Atlantic Coast with those on the Pacific Coast. In History class, you may be asked to compare the culture of the Plains Indians with that of the Native Americans of the West Coast.

Traditionally, comparing has meant focusing on similarities. But today, comparing is widely accepted as including similarities and differences. Contrasting, however, means concentrating on differences only. Frequently, questions will be phrased as follows: "Compare and/or contrast the foreign policies of Canada and the United States between the two World Wars." In a question of this type, you may focus on either similarities or differences or on a combination of similarities and differences. Other questions may be very specific such as: "Contrast the roles of the Canadian prime minister and the American president."

Teachers may have different approaches to comparative assignments. It is especially important to discuss the following questions with your teacher before you start preparing a comparative project:

- Clarify terms like "compare" and "contrast."
- How many sources should be used?
- Should the sources be documented?
- Should the sources be listed?
- How long should the essay be?
- How should the essay be structured?

The process that is described in the following pages can be applied to comparative assignments in most subjects. Let us assume you are studying the topic "Government and Politics in North America" in class. Your teacher has set a short essay on Canadian and American systems of government. The purpose of the assignment is to: "Compare and/or contrast the Canadian and American systems of government."

The teacher has established the following requirements for this short essay:

- Two sources should be used (one Canadian, the other American).
- Encyclopedia articles should be used for the preparatory reading.
- No documentation is needed.
- A list of the sources (Bibliography) is required.
- The length should be between 700 and 800 words. In other words, this is not a major research project.

We will use this example on Canadian and American systems of government to illustrate how to prepare and present a comparative essay.

The route map on this page shows the preparation stages of your "comparative journey." Each stage is illustrated from our example. You will notice that the process is similar to the method that you would use for preparing a report or an essay.

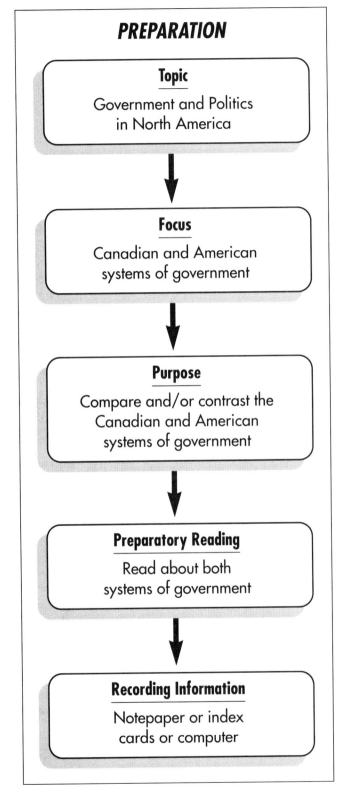

PREPARATION

Topic
Government and Politics in North America

Focus
Canadian and American systems of government

Purpose
Compare and/or contrast the Canadian and American systems of government

Preparatory Reading
Read about both systems of government

Recording Information
Notepaper or index cards or computer

PREPARATION

Preparatory reading is essential for a comparative essay. You must have a thorough understanding of **both** issues to be compared before you start recording information. Encyclopedia articles are especially useful for preparatory reading because they offer a broad survey of the issue. In our example, you would read through the encyclopedia articles to familiarize yourself with the two systems of government. As you read, keep the purpose of your assignment (comparing and/or contrasting) uppermost in your mind. During the preparatory reading, familiarize yourself with the focus of your comparison, and also try to establish similarities and differences. If, however, your purpose is to contrast then you would concentrate on indentifying just differences.

The purpose of our example is to "Compare and/or contrast Canadian and American systems of government," and therefore you would be trying to identify connections that represent similarities **and** differences. These similarities and differences should be noted on separate pages in your *Ideas and Questions Journal*. We have included examples on this page showing how similarities and differences in Canadian and American systems of government could be listed.

Do not bypass the preparatory reading stage because the invisible foundations are even more important for a comparative essay than for the single focus essay. Once you have a good grasp of both issues to be compared and a tentative list of similarities and differences, you are ready to move to the next stage.

Use your library searching skills to locate the required sources. Sign them out of the library in preparation for recording the information. Even though you are not conducting research in a number of sources, **you still need a system for recording your ideas and information.** You can use notepaper, index cards, or a computer. These methods are described in detail on the following pages.

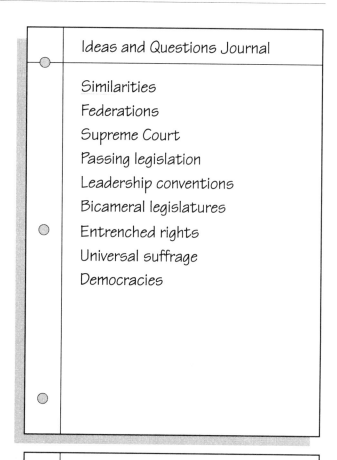

Ideas and Questions Journal

Similarities
Federations
Supreme Court
Passing legislation
Leadership conventions
Bicameral legislatures
Entrenched rights
Universal suffrage
Democracies

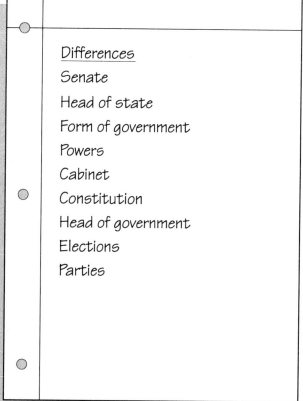

Differences
Senate
Head of state
Form of government
Powers
Cabinet
Constitution
Head of government
Elections
Parties

Notepaper Method

Set up notepaper pages headed "Similarities" and "Differences" as shown below and on the following page. You will note that the columns are set up differently on each page. You already have a tentative list of similarities and differences in your *Ideas and Questions Journal* as a starting point. Read carefully through your first source, looking for information that represents either a similarity or a difference in Canadian and American government. Record the information on either the similarities or differences page. List the main points in the similarities or differences column. List the explanatory details and examples in the adjoining columns. There must be corresponding examples and details from both Canada and the United States to make a comparison possible. **You cannot compare something with nothing.**

Read carefully through your next source looking for similarities and differences, and record the

Similarities	Canada / United States
Supreme Court	interprets the constitution
Federation	provinces and states
Entrenched rights	Charter of Rights and Bill of Rights
Senate	same name; protects provinces and states
Money bills	start in Commons and House of Representatives
Democracies	universal suffrage
Bicameral	Commons and Senate; House of Representatives and Senate
Committees	important part of legislative process
Legislation	three readings in each house
Cabinet	supervises departments
Supreme Court	nine judges including a Chief Justice
Constitution	partly written in Canada; entirely written in United States

details as just explained. Your sources (unless they are comparative studies) will not provide you with the similarities and differences. You will have to establish the connections from your reading. Read your sources carefully, apply your creative imagination as you search for connections. Then record the information on your notepaper as shown.

Since our example is not a major research paper and you are not required to document your sources, there is no need to indicate the source of each note with a code. However, if you wish to code your sources, you should use index cards. There is insufficient space on the notepaper for source codes and page references, but index cards provide the necessary space. See the next page for an example.

Write on one side of the notepaper and leave a line between each note. This will enable you to separate the individual notes with scissors later when you are ready to start structuring your answer.

Canada	Differences	United States
appointed by P.M.; 104 members	Senate	elected; (2 X 50=100)
constitutional monarchy	Form of government	republic
monarch, governor-general	Head of state	president
elected and responsible to Commons	Cabinet	not in Congress, appointed by president
prime minister, elected member of Commons	Head of government	president, may not sit in Congress
within five years	Elections	fixed terms
weak	Senate	powerful
vote of no-confidence	Removal of head of government	impeach
P.M. controls. Commons and Senate seldom deadlocked. P.M. and Cabinet responsible for failure.	Legislation	president no control. Senate and reps. often deadlocked. President and Cabinet not responsible for failure.
unlimited terms	Head of government	two terms
not influential	Senate (legislation)	important

Index Card Method

You can use index cards for recording your information instead of notepaper. Each main point should be written on a separate card with a heading and the corresponding details and examples. Indicate next to the heading whether it is a similarity (S) or a difference (D). Read the previous section on the notepaper method because the instructions for recording the information are not repeated here.

There is no need to indicate the source for each note because our example is not a major research paper. However, it is very easy to include the source code and page reference as we have shown in the "Cabinet" example on this page.

Sometimes it is quicker and more effective to use diagrams rather than text to demonstrate a similarity or a difference. See the example below. It shows overlapping powers in Canada and the separation of powers in the United States.

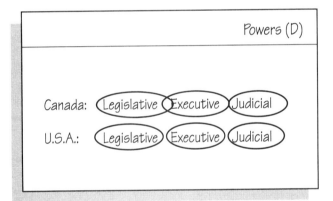

> Legislation (D)
>
> Canada - P.M. controls. Commons and Senate seldom deadlocked. P.M. and Cabinet responsible for failure.
>
> U.S.A. - president no control. Senate and reps. often deadlocked. President and Cabinet not responsible for failure.

> Senate (S)
>
> Same name. Protects provinces and states.

> Cabinet (D)
>
> Canada — Selected by P.M. from elected members of ⌐(BP31) House of Commons
>
> U.S.A. — Selected by president from outside Congress ⌐(CGT6)
>
> └─── **Source Code and Page**

Y ou can also use a computer for recording the information for a comparative essay. Set up notepaper or index card files as explained in the essay section on page 42.

PRESENTATION

If you are using notepaper, take a pair of scissors and separate the notes. **Keep the "Similarities" and "Differences" notes apart.** Next, group the notepaper strips into major categories. For example, all notes about differences between the Canadian and American Senates should be grouped as shown below.

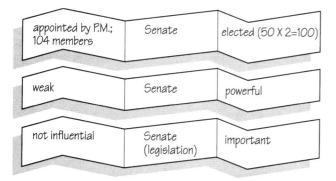

Work through your "Differences" notes grouping all notes with common headings like the "Senate" example above. Use paper clips to keep them together.

Once you have arranged your "Differences," go through your "Similarities" notestrips and group them under common headings as shown below.

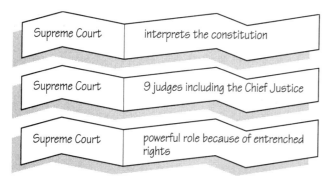

Follow exactly the same method if you used index cards. Each card will have a heading followed by an (S) or a (D). It is easy to group them by common headings like the notestrips.

Do not mix similarities and differences in one group. In other words, notes dealing with differences between the Senates should be kept separate from those dealing with similarities in the Senate. There is no need to identify each notestrip with an (S) or a (D) because the different column arrangements clearly distinguish the similarities from the differences.

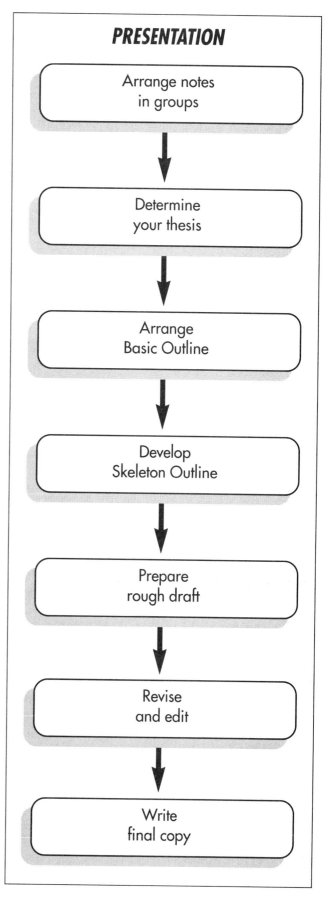

Once you have grouped your notes, decide whether major similarities or major differences are more common. Perhaps there is an equal mix of similarities and differences. **These are important considerations because they will determine your thesis and the structure of your answer.**

After grouping your notes, you may find that one section has far more information than all the others. For example, you may have so much information (both similarities and differences) on the Senate that you may wish to focus your essay just on the Canadian and American Senates. **However, do not narrow the focus of your comparison unless your teacher has approved the change.**

In our example, there were considerably more important differences than similarities. It is logical then to focus the essay on the major differences between Canadian and American systems of government. The next step is to select the most important differences from our grouped notes to illustrate our thesis that Canadian and American systems of government are different and distinctive.

You would choose the major differences from your groups of notes to form the body of the comparative essay. These major differences would be set up in the Basic Outline as shown opposite. Once the Basic Outline is established, the next step is to structure the Skeleton Outline. In exactly the same way as described in the report (page 19) and the essay (page 46), you would read through the notes of each section of the Basic Outline separately. Then you would choose the relevant information needed to develop the comparison for each section. Remember, **there must be corresponding examples from both sides of your issue** (in our example Canadian and American systems of government) **to make comparisons.**

Since our example is a short assignment (700–800 words), a Skeleton Outline would provide sufficient supporting detail for the essay. If you need more detail, continue to the Point-form Outline stage as explained in the report and essay sections.

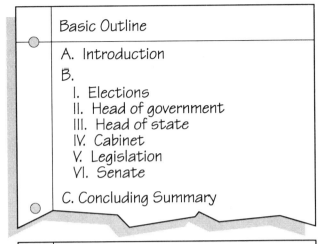

Basic Outline

A. Introduction
B.
   I. Elections
   II. Head of government
   III. Head of state
   IV. Cabinet
   V. Legislation
   VI. Senate
C. Concluding Summary

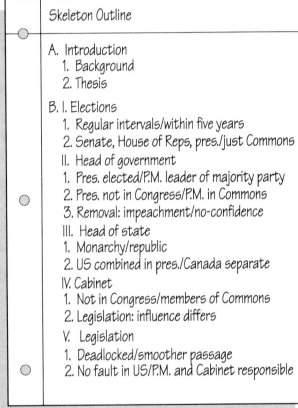

Skeleton Outline

A. Introduction
   1. Background
   2. Thesis

B. I. Elections
   1. Regular intervals/within five years
   2. Senate, House of Reps, pres./just Commons
  II. Head of government
   1. Pres. elected/P.M. leader of majority party
   2. Pres. not in Congress/P.M. in Commons
   3. Removal: impeachment/no-confidence
  III. Head of state
   1. Monarchy/republic
   2. US combined in pres./Canada separate
  IV. Cabinet
   1. Not in Congress/members of Commons
   2. Legislation: influence differs
  V. Legislation
   1. Deadlocked/smoother passage
   2. No fault in US/P.M. and Cabinet responsible

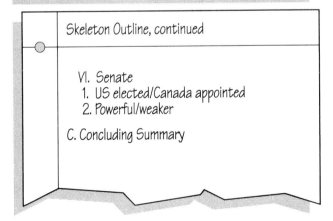

Skeleton Outline, continued

  VI. Senate
   1. US elected/Canada appointed
   2. Powerful/weaker

C. Concluding Summary

As in the report and the essay, the Outlines provide a formula for developing the paragraphs. In a short comparative essay such as our example, the Basic Outline will set up the paragraph structure. The Skeleton Outline will provide the supporting detail as shown opposite. (In a longer comparative term paper, you would use the Point-form Outline for your paragraphs as explained in the report and essay sections.) Once you have your structure mapped out with the supporting detail, it is easy to write your rough draft. Remember:

- Write clearly and correctly.
- Introduce the essay clearly.
- Organize paragraphs around a central focal point.
- Demonstrate similarities and/or differences with examples in the body.
- Include information or observations relevant to your thesis.
- Sum up your conclusions in the final paragraph.
- Revise and edit the rough draft.

A comparative study is not a report — it is an essay with a thesis. Therefore, you cannot just describe whatever you are comparing, such as Canadian and American systems of government; you have to demonstrate the connections and relationships clearly. You cannot expect your readers to figure out the connections.

A complete sample essay is shown on pages 70–71. You will notice that it has an Introduction with a clear statement of thesis (differences dominate the two systems of government). The body is developed around the structure of the Outlines. There is a short Concluding Summary. A Title Page and a Bibliography have also been provided.

Skeleton Outline

A. Introduction
    1. Background   (paragraph)
    2. Thesis   (paragraph)

B. I. Elections   (paragraph)
    1. Regular intervals/within five years
    2. Senate, House of Reps, pres./just Commons

II. Head of government   (paragraph)
    1. Pres. elected/P.M. leader of majority party
    2. Pres. not in Congress/P.M. in Commons
    3. Removal: impeachment/no-confidence

III. Head of state   (paragraph)
    1. Monarchy/republic
    2. US combined in pres./Canada separate

IV. Cabinet   (paragraph)
    1. Not in Congress/members of Commons
    2. Legislation—influence differs

V. Legislation   (paragraph)
    1. Deadlocked/smoother passage
    2. No fault in US/P.M. and Cabinet responsible

VI. Senate   (paragraph)
    1. US elected/Canada appointed
    2. Powerful/weaker

C. Concluding Summary   (paragraph)

The Americans successfully fought a revolutionary war against the British to gain their independence. In 1787, they designed a distinctly American Constitution. Canada, on the other hand, followed a peaceful and evolutionary route. In the slow process of advancing to independence, Canada adopted many features of British Parliamentary government.

Although Canada and the United States of America have common characteristics, history has shaped two different and distinctive systems of government.

Elections are one major difference. The Americans hold biennial federal elections in November. The House of Representatives and one-third of the Senate are elected every two years. The president is elected every four years. In Canada elections are not held at fixed intervals. The Constitution requires that an election must be called within five years of the previous election. In a federal election members are elected to the House of Commons only. American elections are called at fixed times for specified terms, unlike the more flexible Canadian system.

The roles of the prime minister and the president as heads of government are also different. In Canada, the prime minister is the leader of the party that controls the most seats in the House of Commons. By tradition the prime minister must be an elected member of the Commons. The president is elected directly by the people but is not permitted to sit in either house of Congress. The only way to remove an American president is by impeachment, but a Canadian prime minister can be forced to resign by a vote of no-confidence in the House of Commons.

Another difference between the two forms of government is that Canada is a constitutional monarchy, while the United States is a republic. The Americans have combined the positions of head of state and head of government in the presidency. In Canada the positions are separate: the monarch, represented by the governor-general, is head of state and the prime minister is head of government. However, it is the prime minister who actually chooses the governor-general. The president and prime minister may have different roles, but they are both powerful figures.

Although the Cabinets are appointed by the president and prime minister and Cabinet members administer the government departments, the similarities stop there. Like the president, the American Cabinet is not permitted to sit in Congress. This allows the president to select experts from all over the country. In Canada, the prime minister is required by tradition to select the Cabinet from the elected members of the House of Commons. As members of the Commons, the Canadian Cabinet have an influential role in shaping and passing the laws. The appointed American Cabinet does not have the same power in shaping legislation.

Although the process of passing bills into law is similar, there are other legislative differences. Since the prime minister and Cabinet launch the bills in a house that they control, they can usually guide these bills through fairly easily. The Canadian Senate may stall a bill, but will seldom reject it outright. The governor-general automatically signs into law all bills passed by both houses. Passage of legislation in the United States is seldom as smooth a process. Legislation is often deadlocked for months because control of Congress and the presidency may be in the hands of different parties. A law in its final form may be very different to the original bill. The prime minister and Cabinet have more power than their American counterparts in passing legislation. There is a price though: if a major bill fails to pass in the Commons, the prime minister and Cabinet have to resign and another election is called. Failure of a bill in Congress cannot be blamed on the president and Cabinet.

Other than the name, the two Senates have very little in common. The one hundred members of the American Senate (two representatives per state) are elected for a term of six years each. One-third of the Senate is elected every two years so that the composition of the membership is rotated. Canadian Senators (104) are appointed by the prime minister to serve until they reach seventy-five years of age. American Senators can block and strike down bills, while the Canadian Senate can really only stall legislation. Furthermore, the American Constitution has given the Senate powers such as approving all foreign treaties. The elected American Senate representing all the states equally is a more powerful body than the appointed Canadian Senate.

Increasingly Canada is influenced by American cultural values, but the past still has an enduring influence on our political system. Although there are some similarities between our systems of government, differences still dominate in the most important aspects of government in the United States and Canada.

A Comparative Study of Government in Canada and the United States

Judy Sandler
Social Studies 2A
Ms. Helen Thexton
June 1993

Bibliography

Beaudoin, G.A. "Constitutional Law." *The Canadian Encyclopedia*. 1988 ed.

Harris, James T. "United States of America: The Structure of Government." *Encyclopaedia Britannica: Macropaedia*. 15th ed.

Merritt, Allen S. and George W. Brown. *Canadians and their Government*. 2nd ed. Toronto: Fitzhenry and Whiteside, 1983.

Skidmore, Max J. and Marshall C. Wanke. *American Government: A Brief Introduction*. 3rd ed. New York: St. Martin's Press, 1981.

5 TIPS ON STYLE

Style is the manner in which you use language, the way you express yourself. It is not what you write but how you write. Following these "tips" will result in a more polished, clearly written final product.

- **Use simple and direct language.** Avoid fancy words when plain words will serve your purpose. If you can say it more simply, you should do so. If you are describing a mollusk that has dark and light stripes, do not say it has "alternating tenebrious and canescent bands." Say it is striped like a zebra.

- **Eliminate vague words.** If it is unclear what you are trying to say, replace the word or words with more definite ones. For example, "The zebra mussel is a small striped creature," is not as precise as "The zebra mussel is a brown and white mollusk about 2.5 cm in length." By replacing the vague words "small," "striped," and "creature" with more concrete words, the reader has a much better picture of the zebra mussel.

- **Omit needless words.** Every word in a sentence should serve a purpose. If a word seems unnecessary, try to eliminate or replace it. For example, "In spite of the fact that . . ." can be stated more simply as "Although . . ."

- **Check the fluency of your writing.** Good writing has an even, easy flow. When read aloud, it should flow naturally off your tongue. If you have difficulty reading it, revise it. Using linking words such as "therefore" and "consequently" can improve the rhythm of your writing.

- **Keep your tone formal.** The tone of your report or essay is how you express your own voice in your writing. Because reports and essays are serious pieces of writing, your tone should be formal. Therefore, you should not use casual or slang language that you might use with your friends. For example, you would not write this: "When the zebra mussels came here they made all kinds of problems for the fish and clams and stuff." The point would be better expressed this way: "The arrival of the zebra mussels in North America created a major upset in the aquatic life of the Great Lakes."

- **Use active verbs instead of passive verbs.** Active verbs are more forceful and concise than passive verbs. It is better to state "Zebra mussels *invaded* the Great Lakes" than "The Great Lakes *were invaded by* zebra mussels."

- **Make sure those active verbs are consistent in tense.** Reports and essays are usually written in the past tense. Do not shift from "is" to "was" and from "are" to "were" throughout the essay.

- **Avoid using contractions.** Using words such as "do not" instead of "don't" or "cannot" in place of "can't" keeps your writing formal. You will notice that this guide does not use contractions.

- **Check for correct spelling.** Keep a dictionary at your side to help you when you are unsure of the spelling of a word. If you are using a computer, make use of the spell check functions but do not rely on them entirely. Remember that a computer cannot tell whether you should use "too," "two," or "to."

- **Choose your words carefully.** The development and clear expression of an idea depends largely on your selection and use of words. A dictionary and a thesaurus will help you expand your vocabulary. A thesaurus or dictionary of synonyms will help you replace words. Instead of repeatedly using the verb "trade," you could replace it occasionally with words like "barter" or "exchange."

- **Vary the length of your sentences.** Mixing longer sentences with shorter ones changes the pace of your writing. This will liven up your writing. Shorter sentences can be used to give emphasis and effect to a point.

- **Choose your pronouns carefully.** Although instructional guides such as this one often use the pronouns "you" and "we," avoid using "you" or "we" and use "I" sparingly in your projects. Some teachers object to the use of "I," so always consult your teacher. Instead of "I" some teachers prefer "the author" or "the writer."

- **Use abbreviations carefully.** You may use abbreviations such as UN for the United Nations, as long as you identify them the first time you use them.

- **Pay attention to your punctuation.** Proper punctuation will make your sentences flow and help clarify the meaning of your ideas.

- **Avoid sexist language.** Do not use language that excludes women. Saying "An American Senator is usually the best man for the job because he is elected by the people" excludes all female senators. It is better to rephrase the sentence as follows: "Because American senators are elected by the people, they are usually the most suitable for the job." Sometimes it is just a matter of substituting a word like police officer for policeman. There are books available to help you choose nonsexist words and phrases — ask your teacher-librarian.

Writers are not born; they develop their craft through reading widely and practising their writing constantly. Developing your writing skills is no different from perfecting any skills — it requires effort and practice.

6 CONCLUDING SUMMARY

This guide has taken you step by step through the process of researching and presenting reports, essays, and comparative essays. We have provided you with the basic provisions and skills that you will need to complete your assignments. This is the end of this stage of your journey.

As you plan and write your projects, you will be setting your own directions and plotting your own routes. With proper provisions, practice, and experience, you will soon become a stronger researcher and writer. By developing your skills you can reach your destination in less time with less effort.

You should learn from the experience of each journey. When your essays and reports are returned to you by your teacher, do not flip through them and then throw them away.

- Read your teacher's comments carefully.

- Discuss any comments that are unclear to you with your teacher.
- Read the best essays and reports in your class to see how they differ from yours.
- Write a personal assessment of your project.
- Make a list of weaknesses to address in your next project. Read this list before starting each project.
- Keep all your essays and reports to mark your progress.

Every report or essay that you write is a journey of exploration and discovery. You will learn about yourself, you will learn about your topic, and you will learn skills ranging from cooperating with other students to library research techniques. Take the knowledge and the experience with you and make each journey more fulfilling than the last.

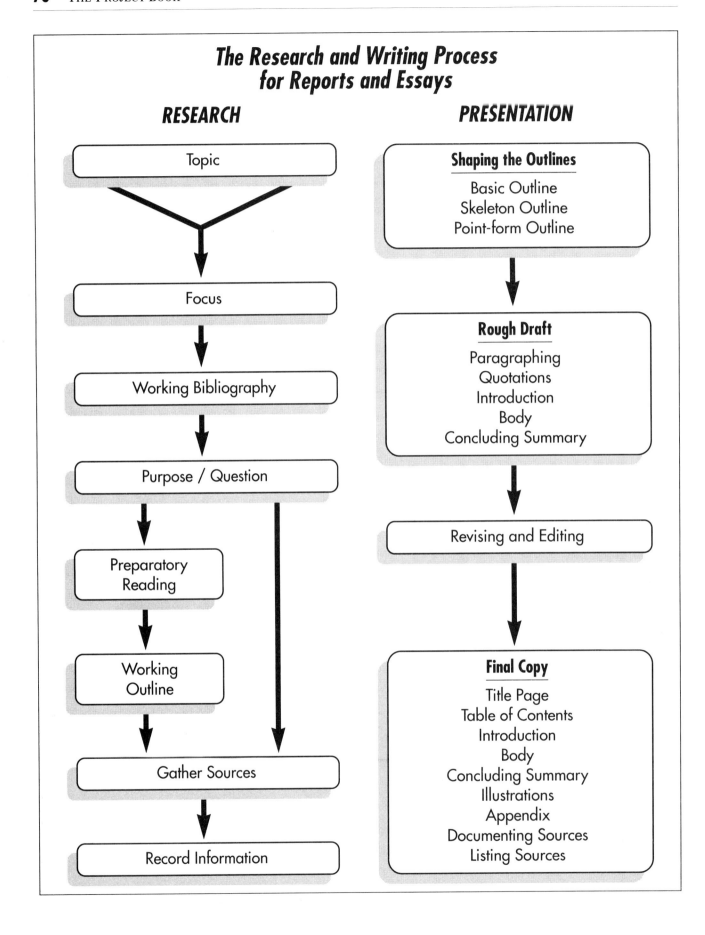

The Research and Writing Process for Reports and Essays

RESEARCH

Topic

Focus

Working Bibliography

Purpose / Question

Preparatory Reading

Working Outline

Gather Sources

Record Information

PRESENTATION

Shaping the Outlines
Basic Outline
Skeleton Outline
Point-form Outline

Rough Draft
Paragraphing
Quotations
Introduction
Body
Concluding Summary

Revising and Editing

Final Copy
Title Page
Table of Contents
Introduction
Body
Concluding Summary
Illustrations
Appendix
Documenting Sources
Listing Sources

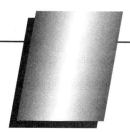

APPENDIX

1. ORAL PRESENTATIONS

If your project is to be an oral presentation, it is still necessary to do the preparatory work. There is no major difference in the preparation of an oral and a written assignment up to the Point-form Outline stage. Like written assignments, oral presentations can be either reports or essays. An oral essay is often known as a seminar or viewpoint and like a written essay, you would have to develop and demonstrate an argument or thesis or point of view. An oral report is informative and explanatory and does not present an argument or point of view. Make sure that you know in advance whether you are to present an oral report or a seminar.

Once you have shaped your Point-form Outline, you are ready to start rehearsing your presentation. There is no need to write or type a rough copy — that might encourage you to memorize or read it. If you memorize your report, you may sound like a robot, and if you forget a crucial point you may panic. Simply reading it may put your audience to sleep.

You will be adequately prepared for your presentation if you have converted your research into a concise Point-form Outline. You will have the essential information structured according to the ABC formula. You should be able to communicate it to your audience without reading or memorizing it. Some people write their points on cue cards (index cards), but you could run into trouble if you drop a card or they get out of order.

A different method is to write your Point-form Outline on a page of notepaper (and on the reverse side if necessary) and to refer to it while you address your audience. You could even cut the page in half if you prefer a smaller piece of paper. Even better, reduce your Point-form Outline to key words and write it on a large (13 x 20 cm) index card or a firm piece of white cardboard. Circle the main sections and highlight the subsections for quick and easy reference. You can also jot down suggestions in the margin for delivery such as where to pause or where to repeat important information.

Rehearsing is important for oral presentations. You may want to persuade some friends to act as an audience and comment on your presentation. Tape-recording your presentation and then playing it back allows you to detect flaws in your oral delivery. Rehearsing in front of a mirror shows you how you are presenting yourself. Look at what your "body language" is saying and improve on it if necessary. A video recording will allow you to review your entire performance and fine tune it. Careful rehearsing will not only improve your presentation but will give you a sense of confidence.

Communicating your message to your audience is your most important task. Keep these points in mind to help make your presentation run smoothly.

- Use appropriate language for a formal presentation.
- Choose your words carefully to make sure they are effective.
- Pronounce your words clearly.
- Try to alternate between loud and soft levels of voice for emphasis.
- Make sure your delivery is not too fast or too slow.
- Pause occasionally at important points to give them emphasis.
- Maintain eye contact with your audience.
- Stand (or sit) erect.
- Use humour sparingly.
- Be confident. Remember, you are the expert.
- Be enthusiastic.

Visual aids can give added impact to your presentation. For example, you could illustrate a point by showing a graph on an overhead projector. The next section lists a variety of presentation techniques, and you may wish to use some of them. However, you must keep the spotlight on yourself. Do not let technology become the focus of your presentation. To keep the audience attentive to what you are saying, do not hand out material during your presentation. Distribute it when you are finished.

2. MULTIMEDIA PRESENTATIONS

You might want to supplement your presentations with different approaches and equipment. A variety of options are available and we have listed a selection below. Many of these, such as slides, can be generated on computer. Computers will also mix sound and video images. Knowing how to use multimedia equipment is a useful skill today. But remember that your main purpose is to convey your message to your audience. Do not try to overwhelm them with technological wizardry.

- Chalkboard
- Charts
- Posters
- Handouts
- Maps
- Photographs
- Overhead transparencies
- Video
- Filmstrips
- Slides
- Sound synchronization with slides
- Guest speakers
- Music
- Tape-recordings
- Simulations/role play
- Costumes
- Opaque projector
- Film
- Laser disc
- Computer with CD-ROM player

3. ILLUSTRATIONS

There are two major types of illustrations: tables and figures. Tables contain statistical data, while figures consist of photographs, maps, drawings, graphs, diagrams, charts, and pictures. Software such as spreadsheets or graphics programs allow you to do most illustrations on computer. If computer facilities are not available, tables and figures can still be prepared by hand. Aim for clarity and simplicity when laying out your illustrations. Demonstrated in the following pages are some of the more commonly used illustrations.

Tables

Statistical tables are either set in the relevant place in the text or placed in the Appendix. Each table is assigned a concise title and a number. The source of the information must also be given. Keep your tables simple and include only the essential statistical information. Tables must not be included just to fill space. The data in each table must be explained carefully in the text of a report or linked clearly to the development of the thesis in an essay. An example of a table is shown below.

Table 1. Elevations, Areas, and Depths of the Great Lakes					
LAKE	ELEVATION (m)	LENGTH (km)	BREADTH (km)	MAXIMUM DEPTH (m)	TOTAL AREA (km^2)
Superior	184	563	257	405	84 243
Michigan	176	494	190	281	57 575
Huron	177	332	295	229	63 096
Erie	174	388	92	64	25 812
Ontario	75	311	85	244	19 001

Source: Adapted from *Canada Yearbook 1992* (Ottawa: Statistics Canada, 1991), 29. Reproduced with the permission of the Minister of Industry, Science and Technology, 1993.

Figures

Like tables, figures are placed either in the body or in the Appendix. Figures are numbered consecutively. Titles, sometimes accompanied by a brief explanation, are usually placed below the figure. The source of the information must also be given. Any symbols must be explained in a legend and placed within the figure.

Graphic illustrations are useful for showing complex statistical information in a clear and simple way. The various types of illustrations have different purposes, and you should choose carefully when deciding on your charts and graphs. Ensure that each one is relevant to your report or essay.

Maps

Bear these points in mind when you are constructing your maps:

- Place a margin around the map.
- Indicate orientation using the north point.
- Use a concise title.
- Provide the scale in linear or representative fraction form.
- Use conventional symbols, such as ++++ for a railway line.
- Explain symbols and colours in a key or legend.
- Concentrate on neatness and simplicity if you are doing the map by hand.
- Consider using computer cartographic programs for your maps.

Figure 1 The Great Lakes

Organizational Charts

Organizational Charts, sometimes called Flow Charts, show systems, structures, or processes. We have used charts throughout this guide to simplify the research and writing process by representing it diagramatically.

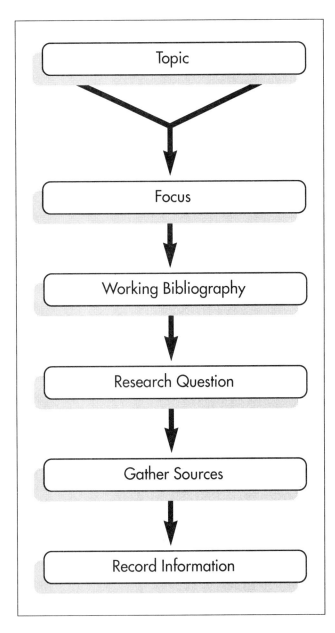

Line Graphs

Line graphs are used to show changing trends over a period of time. Line graphs are plotted on a rectangular grid with two axes or scales. Grid lines are often omitted from the completed graph. The horizontal axis usually represents time in years and the vertical axis usually represents a value such as dollars.[4] Work out a vertical and horizontal scale that will enable you to fit the graph comfortably on the page. Do not make it too small and do not clutter the graph with unnecessary detail. Simplicity and accuracy should be your aim.

Plot the data on the grid and then link the points. You can either use straight lines joining the points or curved lines that fit the general trend of the points. Balance the graph by ensuring that the lines or curves run through the centre of the graph.[5]

Some graphs are single-line graphs, while others have multiple lines or curves. You may use symbols with a legend to identify the lines or you may use solid, broken, or dotted lines instead. You must label the lines if you do not use a legend. If you have intersecting lines or curves on a graph then limit the lines or curves to three. If there are no intersections, five should be the maximum number of lines on a graph. It is better to construct another graph than confuse the reader with extensive detail.

Descriptors for the vertical axes are usually placed parallel to the axis as we have shown in our examples. It is also acceptable to place these descriptors horizontally.

Examples of line graphs are shown on the next page.

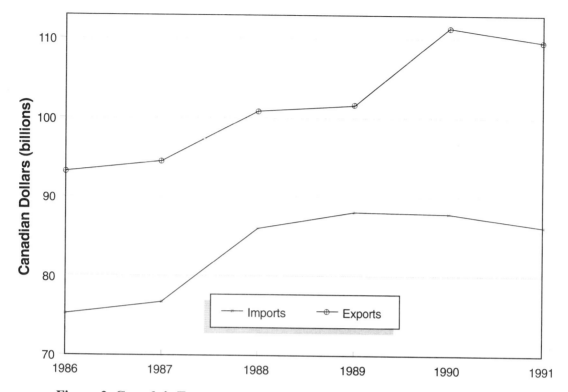

Figure 2. Canada's Export–Import Trade with the United States.
Source: Department of External Affairs and International Trade, Ottawa.

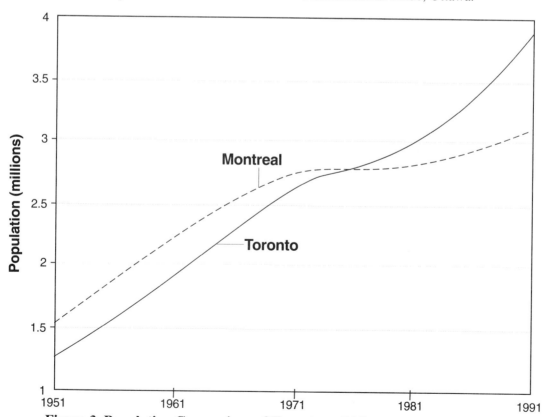

Figure 3. Population Comparison of Toronto and Montreal.
Source: John Robert Colombo, ed. *The Canadian Global Almanac.*
(Toronto: Macmillan Canada, 1992), 53.

Bar/Column Charts

Traditionally, "bar" charts have referred to horizontal organization, while "column" charts represented vertical structure. The term bar chart is more commonly used today for both vertical and horizontal illustrations.

Bar charts are simple to construct and easy to use. They are especially useful for showing comparisons at a specified time.[6] You can use single bars or double bars as shown in the examples. Normally, you can use either horizontal or vertical organization in a bar chart. See below for examples of each.

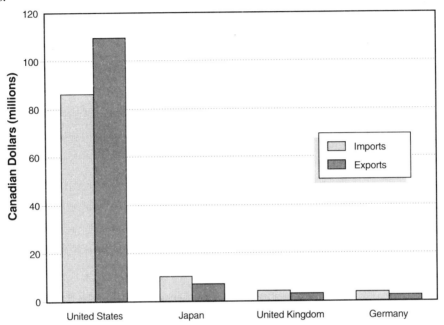

Figure 4. Canada's Main Trading Partners, 1991.
Source: Economic Planning Division, External Affairs, Canada.

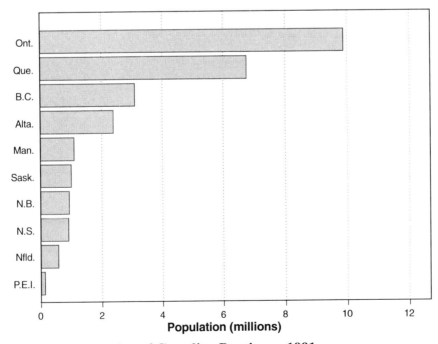

Figure 5. Population of Canadian Provinces, 1991.
Source: John Robert Colombo, ed. *The Canadian Global Almanac.*
(Toronto: Macmillan Canada, 1992), 40.

Circle Charts

Divided circle charts are usually called "pie" charts. They are useful for showing the relationship between different parts of a category such as energy. There should be no more than six divisions or "slices" of the pie, because the segments will become too small. Constructing a pie chart requires some calculations. Each element has to be converted to a percentage if it is not in percentage form. The percentage must then be converted to degrees (360° in a circle). A protractor and a compass will be needed if you are constructing the chart by hand.[7] Most computer spreadsheet programs will do the calculation and construction of the chart automatically.

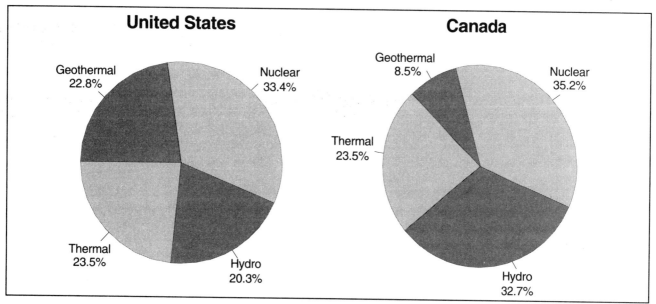

Figure 6. Sources of Energy in Canada and the United States.
Source: *1990 Energy Statistics Yearbook* (New York: United Nations, 1990), 386.

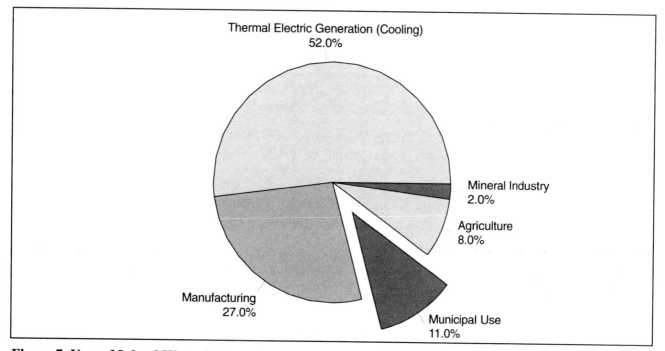

Figure 7. Uses of Inland Water in Canada.
Source: Adapted from *Canada Yearbook 1992* (Ottawa: Statistics Canada, 1991), 20. Reproduced with the permission of the Ministry of Industry, Science and Technology, 1993.

Climate Graphs

Climate graphs, often called climographs, are widely used in geography. Climate graphs combine line graphs and vertical bars. A line graph is used to show average monthly temperatures. A bar chart reflects average monthly precipitation. Spaces nor-mally appearing between the vertical columns in a bar chart are eliminated in a climate graph. The months of the year are entered on the horizontal axis. The left vertical axis is used for temperature degrees. The precipitation scale in millimetres of water is placed on the right-hand vertical axis.

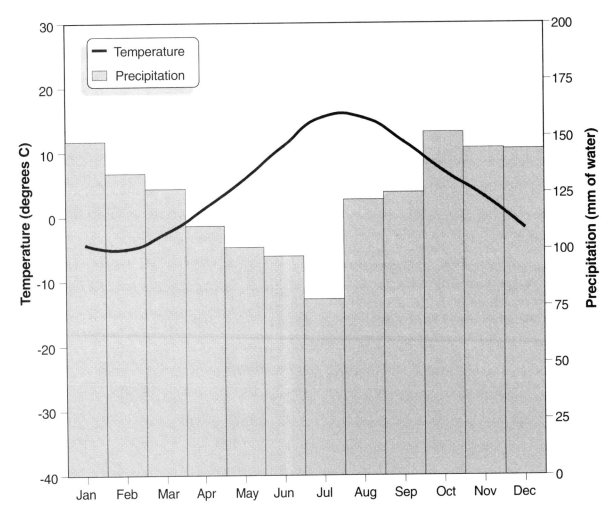

Figure 8. Climate of St. John's, 1942–1990.
Source: *Canadian Climate Normals 1961–1990.* Environment Canada. April 1993.

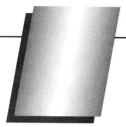

GLOSSARY

Analyzing Examining the material carefully in accordance with the question or purpose, then isolating relevant details and identifying important ideas.

Appendix A section of the report or essay where material too lengthy for the body can be placed. The Appendix is placed before the Endnotes (if used) and the Bibliography.

Argument See **Thesis.**

Bibliographic Aids Resources in a library that assist in developing a list of sources. These resources include catalogues, periodical indexes, and databases.

Bibliography Literally a list of books used as sources for an essay or a report. Now commonly used to refer to all types of sources found useful in completing a research assignment.

Brainstorming The process of generating and listing all the possible aspects, features, and questions about a topic.

Catalogue A list of the holdings of a library, accessible either by index cards, computer terminals, or microfiche readers. Catalogues are based either on the Dewey Decimal system or on the Library of Congress system.

Compare Show the connection or relationship between different individuals, events, problems, or institutions by focusing on the similarities and/or differences.

Contrast Show the connection or relationship between different individuals, events, problems, or institutions by focusing on the differences only.

Documentation The process of acknowledging the sources of your quotations, important information, and paraphrased ideas used in your project.[8]

Endnotes A method of documentation where the source is indicated by a number in the text and the details for the source are provided at the end of the essay or report.

Essay A formal piece of writing developed around a central thesis that is supported by evidence, ideas, and reasons.

Exploratory Reading The preliminary reading done on the topic to explore all the possibilities on which to focus the research project.

Feature See **Focus.**

Focus The broad topic must be narrowed to a specific feature, issue, or problem. These subtopics represent the focus for the research.

Footnote A numbered documentation system where the details of the source are provided at the foot (bottom) of the page.

Issue See **Focus.**

Microfiche Small sheets of film containing micro images of sources of information such as out-of-print books and indexes.

Microfilm Reels of 35 mm or 16 mm film containing micro images of sources of information such as documents and newspapers.

Outlines A progressive series of outlines (Working, Basic, Skeleton, and Point-form) are recommended to ensure that the project has order and structure.

Paraphrase Describing a passage from a source or an author's idea in your own words.

Parenthetical Documentation A method of documentation where the source is provided within parentheses (brackets) in the text. APA (American Psychological Association) and MLA (Modern Language Association) are the two most common parenthetical systems.

Periodicals Popular magazines and scholarly journals published weekly, monthly, or quarterly.

Plagiarism The use of someone else's ideas without acknowledgment of the source.

Point of View See **Thesis.**

Preliminary Research The initial stages of the research up to the "Recording Information" stage. The preliminary research lays the necessary groundwork for analyzing and recording the information.

Preparatory Reading The process of reading about the focus of the assignment. The purpose is to learn about the specific issue or feature to be investigated.

Project A general term covering a variety of independent or group assignments. Projects could be as varied as research papers, oral reports, and scrapbooks.

Report The presentation of factual information that is to inform, explain, narrate, or describe. A report does not develop an opinion or point of view.

Research The process of investigating a problem by gathering and analyzing evidence from primary and/or secondary sources.

Research Paper An investigation of a problem or issue based on primary and/or secondary sources and the development and substantiation of a thesis or argument. A research paper may sometimes be a factual report.

Seminar An oral presentation of a thesis or point of view followed by a discussion.

Sources There are two types of sources of information. Primary sources represent material that has not been interpreted by another person.[9] Secondary sources represent another person's interpretation of primary material.

Style The distinctive manner in which you express yourself in written language. It is the individual imprint that you leave or your writing.

Summarizing Reducing information to its essential details in your own words.

Term Paper See **Research Paper.**

Thesis The point of view, opinion, or argument around which your essay is built.

Thesis Statement A concise statement of your thesis, usually placed at the end of the Introduction. The thesis statement is your response to the research question summed up concisely in one or two sentences — it is not the question itself.

Topic The broad subject area assigned or selected for a report or an essay.

Working Bibliography A list of potential sources of information developed as part of the preliminary research. The extent of the Working Bibliography indicates whether enough potential information will be available and the source titles also provide clues for defining the purpose of the assignment.

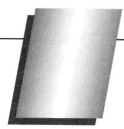

ENDNOTES

[1] Kate Turabian, *Student's Guide for Writing College Papers,* 3rd ed. (Chicago: University of Chicago Press, 1976), 31.

[2] Edward de Bono, *Cort I, Teachers' Notes* (New York: Pergamon, 1973), 7.

[3] Sheridan Baker, *The Practical Stylist,* 7th ed. (New York: Harper, 1990), 43.

[4] Bruce Robertson, *How to Draw Charts and Diagrams* (Cincinnati: North Light Books, 1988), 96.

[5] Ron S. Blicq, *Guidelines for Report Writing,* 2nd ed. (Scarborough, Ontario: Prentice-Hall, 1990), 180–182.

[6] A.J. MacGregor, *Graphics Simplified* (Toronto: University of Toronto Press, 1985), 12.

[7] Robertson 78–79.

[8] Joseph Gibaldi and William S. Achtert, *MLA Handbook for Writers of Research Papers,* 3rd ed. (New York: Modern Language Association, 1988), 155.

[9] *History and Contemporary Studies (O.A.C.): Criteria for Assessment and Evaluation of Student Achievemen* (Toronto: Ontario Ministry of Education, 1992), 2.

BIBLIOGRAPHY

Baker, Sheridan. *The Practical Stylist.* 7th ed. New York: Harper, 1990.

Blicq, Ron S. *Guidelines for Report Writing.* 2nd ed. Scarborough, Ontario: Prentice-Hall, 1990.

de Bono, Edward. *Cort Thinking.* New York: Pergamon, 1973.

_____. *Cort I, Teachers' Notes.* New York: Pergamon, 1973.

Gibaldi, Joseph and William S. Achtert. *MLA Handbook for Writers of Research Papers.* 3rd ed. New York: Modern Language Association, 1988.

Goleman, Daniel et al. *The Creative Spirit.* New York: Dutton, 1992.

MacGregor, A.J. *Graphics Simplified.* Toronto: University of Toronto Press, 1985.

Mann, Thomas. *A Guide to Library Research Methods.* New York: Oxford University Press, 1986.

Robertson, Bruce. *How to Draw Charts and Diagrams.* Cincinnati: North Light Books, 1988.

Robertson, Hugh. *The English Essay: A Guide to Essays and Papers.* Toronto: McGraw-Hill Ryerson, 1993.

Stewart, Kay L. et al. *Essay Writing for Canadian Students.* 2nd ed. Scarborough, Ontario: Prentice-Hall, 1985.

Strunk, William Jr. and E.B. White. *The Elements of Style.* 3rd ed. New York: Macmillan, 1979.

Turabian, Kate L. *A Manual for Writers of Term Papers, Theses, and Dissertations.* 5th ed. Chicago: University of Chicago Press, 1987.

_____. *Student's Guide for Writing College Papers.* 3rd ed. Chicago: University of Chicago Press, 1976.

Zinsser, William. *On Writing Well.* 4th ed. New York: Harper, 1990.